IMAGES
of America

CHILDREN'S HOSPITAL BOSTON

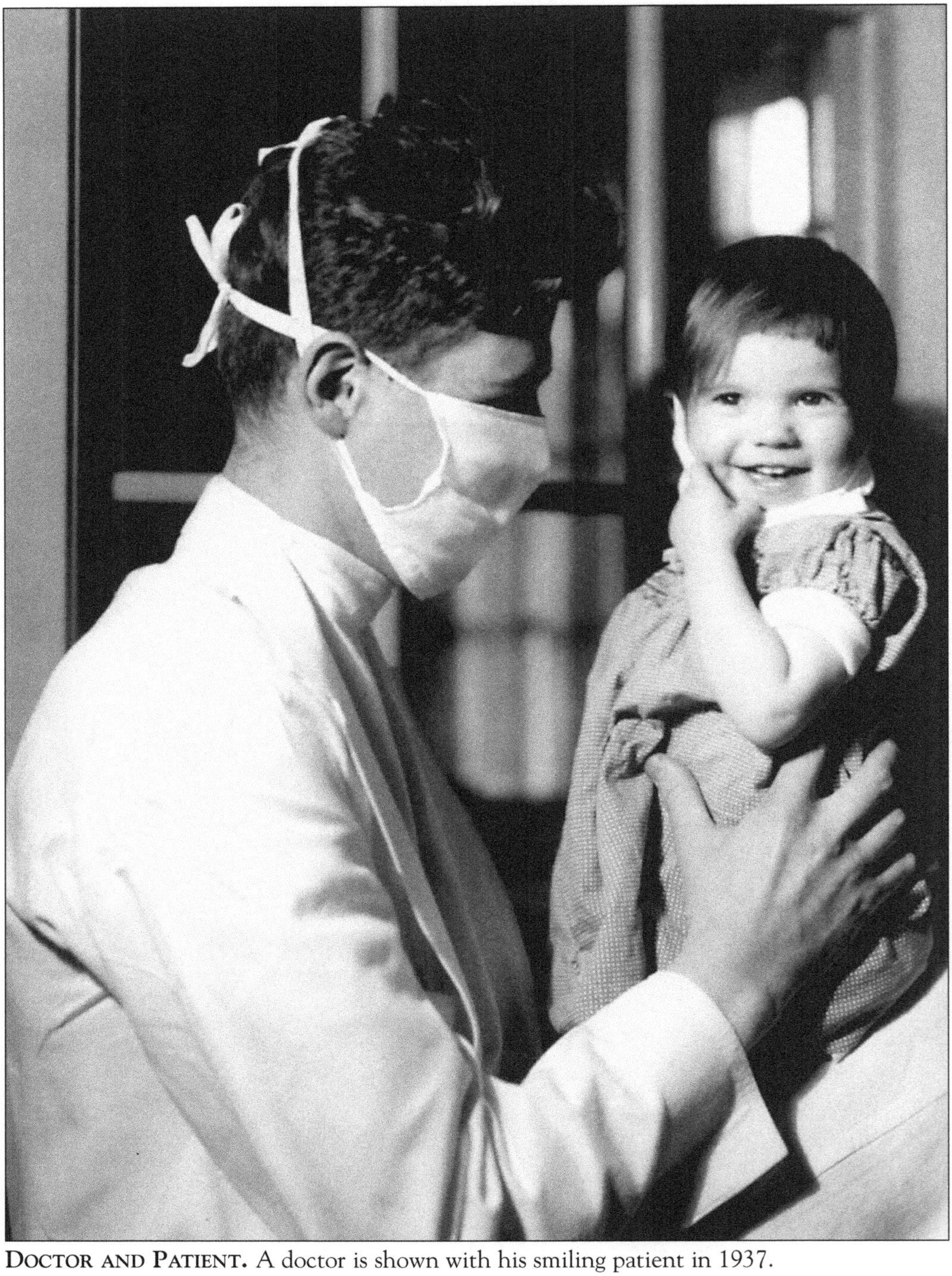

DOCTOR AND PATIENT. A doctor is shown with his smiling patient in 1937.

IMAGES
of America

CHILDREN'S HOSPITAL BOSTON

The Archives Program of
Children's Hospital Boston

ARCADIA
PUBLISHING

ISBN 978-1-5316-2213-8

Published by Arcadia Publishing
Charleston, South Carolina

Library of Congress Catalog Card Number: 2004116479

For all general information contact Arcadia Publishing at:
Telephone 843-853-2070
Fax 843-853-0044
E-mail sales@arcadiapublishing.com
For customer service and orders:
Toll-Free 1-888-313-2665

Visit us on the Internet at www.arcadiapublishing.com

CHILDREN IN THE HOSPITAL.
This photograph was taken *c.* 1940.

CONTENTS

Acknowledgments		6
Introduction		7
1.	A Modest Beginning: Rutland and Washington Streets, 1869–1882	9
2.	A Special Place for Children: Huntington Avenue, 1882–1914	19
3.	Fertile Ground: Longwood Avenue, 1914–1946	35
4.	Friends and Associations: 1869–1946	71
5.	The Development of an International Medical Center: 1946–1990	83
6.	Looking Forward: The 1990s and Beyond	115

Acknowledgments

Healers and the healed are the fabric of a great hospital's history. But the texture of an academic medical center devoted to children is especially rich, interwoven with courageous parents, persistent scientists, and an enormous community of mentors and students, leaders and innovators, philanthropists and administrators, visionaries and volunteers, clinicians and employees.

A good history can only attempt to mirror, somewhat, the richness of their extraordinary efforts and achievements. We therefore acknowledge those who are depicted here and the many who could not be, given the limitations of space. No one should assume that this is the total history of Children's Hospital Boston, when the story of helping just one child often fills volumes of medical records, and the pattern of dedication, discovery, devotion, and optimism of myriad members of the Children's Hospital community is so finely woven.

More directly, this book began as the vision of the Archives Committee of Children's Hospital Boston and its undaunted chairman, who deserve credit not only for the form and persistence of that vision, but for selecting an archivist whose dedication, energy, and focus were essential in implementing the vision in collaboration with others. The committee members are Mark A. Rockoff, MD (chair); Mary Ellen Avery, MD; Patrick Bibbins; Alison Clapp; Estherann Grace, MD; Rudman J. Ham; W. Hardy Hendren, MD; Patricia Hojnowski-Diaz, RN; Jason Larson (archivist); Patrick O'Keefe; David Peck; Mary Radley; Kitty Scott, RN; Phyllis Simpkins; and Anne B. Stone, RN.

Most of the photographs in this book are derived from files in the hospital's archives and its various departments. For their use, and for guidance and moral support in pursuing this project, the editors owe a debt of gratitude to James Mandell, MD, president and chief executive officer, and Sandra Fenwick, chief operating officer, of Children's Hospital Boston.

Many members of the faculty and staff commented and offered suggestions, corrections, images, and other assistance. The editors especially express thanks to the following: members of the Children's Hospital Archives Committee; the Harvard Medical Library in the Francis A. Countway Library of Medicine; the History of Nursing Archives of the Howard Gottlieb Archival Research Center at Boston University; the Boston Public Library; Jessie Barnes; M. Judah Folkman, MD; N. Thorne Griscom, MD; Robert Haggerty, MD; Paul Hickey, MD; David Nathan, MD; Barbara Roach; Fred Rosen, MD; Susan Shaw, RN; Bruce Zetter, PhD; the Children's Hospital School of Nursing Alumnae Association; and the highly talented staff of the Departments of Public Affairs and Media Services. In addition, for their kind, swift assistance in a time of need, we gratefully acknowledge Eleanor Shore, MD, dean for faculty affairs, and Margaret Dale, JD, dean for faculty and research integrity, both of Harvard Medical School.

Royalties from this book will benefit the Archives Endowment Fund of Children's Hospital Boston.

This book was created, written, and edited by an ad hoc committee. Exceptional credit is due to that committee's chair, who led with his legendary diplomacy and kindness. It should be noted that he objected to this acknowledgment, but the rest of the committee, for once, outvoted him.

The Editors

Jason T. Larson, Archivist
Mark A. Rockoff, MD
David R. Breakstone
Patrick Bibbins
Michelle R. Davis
Patrick Taylor, JD
Frederick H. Lovejoy Jr., MD, Chair

Introduction

This is the story of how a tiny hospital for poor urban children grew into one of the nation's largest academic pediatric hospitals and research enterprises housed in a pediatric institution. It is therefore the story of many children, their parents, and the people who cared for them. But it is also a story of the development of pediatrics as a specialty, and of academic pediatric hospitals as medical centers, uniquely designed and operated for children's particular needs.

In the early 19th century, there were very few hospitals in the United States. Children's Hospital Boston began as the labor of love of philanthropists and physicians. Like similar efforts elsewhere, it was created to provide care for ill and needy people who could not afford medical care in their own homes. Most of the early hospitals treated physically or mentally ill adults, though some also admitted a small number of children. Despite the fact that nearly half of all recorded deaths nationwide were young children, few hospitals were devoted especially to their care, and select physicians and civic leaders in Boston were determined to do better.

At Children's Hospital Boston, patients were initially attended by volunteer physicians and religious sisters intent on providing kindness and comfort, despite few effective therapies. During this time, care was generally limited to what compassion, faith, hygiene, and nutrition could effect. Deep knowledge of pediatric diseases and cures was missing, and it would eventually come only through decades of research.

Today, Children's Hospital Boston is a world center for specialized medical and surgical remedies unimaginable when it began. Aside from being palliative, medicine is also scientific, technological, curative, and preventative. Not just children, but families, are treated. Where known cures stop, clinical research offers families hope. A small brick house, the site of the first hospital, has been replaced by a complex, interdependent community the size of a small city. Clinical and research relationships reach across the world into global, national, regional, and community institutions that provide pre-care, post-care, drugs, devices, advanced technology, research laboratories, funding, education and training, public health services, preventative services, community medicine, and family support.

In between the beginning and the present is a story of how pediatrics and pediatric hospitals changed; cures became integrated with discovery, and caring became integrated with the development of specialized healthcare professionals at work in redesigned, high-tech "environments of care" with complicated instrumentation. In moving from the palliative to the therapeutic, and from the descriptive to the scientific, pediatric professionals and hospitals reorganized themselves and the world around them by creating new pediatric departments; training new specialists focused on every aspect of caring for infants, children, adolescents, and young adults; fostering development of pediatric nurses, social workers, medical and surgical technicians, physical and respiratory therapists, and many other premier professionals; uniting basic and clinical sciences to discover and affect the mechanisms of disease and wellness; and expanding their relationships with government and other healthcare and educational institutions around the globe.

This book is a distillation of that story through glimpses of some of the magnificent people who, in placing their skills in the service of children, encouraged and nurtured the many faces of pediatric medicine and surgery; established an enduring institution that would improve the health of countless children locally, regionally, nationally, and internationally; and made Children's Hospital Boston a global leader in discovering the causes and cures of pediatric illness.

In the last chapter, as the story of Children's Hospital spans into the 21st century, the editors faced a new challenge: predicting the future. Now, however, there are so many clinical and scientific leaders in so many fields that it would be impossible to select among them, and history—especially scientific history—is necessarily judged in hindsight. For these reasons, the faces of the future, even as we see them now, must be left to subsequent editions.

THE COMMUNITY FUND. This boy represents the many children who have been helped by Children's Hospital.

One

A MODEST BEGINNING

RUTLAND AND WASHINGTON STREETS, 1869–1882

By 1869, the Civil War had ended and the Gilded Age had begun. As Mark Twain put it, "the flush times were in magnificent flower." In the following decades, industrialization and growing corporate power strained the country's populist foundation, dividing the newly wealthy from the growing numbers of urban poor. Social reformers aligned with philanthropists to address, as they saw it, the moral and physical well-being of poor immigrants and their children.

Medicine was ill-suited to help. In his 1869–1870 annual report, the new president of Harvard College, Charles William Eliot, decried the "ignorance and general incompetency of the average graduate of American Medical Schools, at the time he receives the degree which turns him loose on the community." Experienced physicians were not much better: their crude methods of treating casualties in the Civil War have been compared to the medical practices of the late Middle Ages. Physicians were not necessarily distinguished, in the public mind, from quacks and "resurrection men."

That was to change. Soon after the end of the war, Dr. Francis Henry Brown organized a small group of his fellow Harvard Medical School graduates, along with several prominent civic leaders in Boston, to begin one of the nation's earliest children's hospitals. This followed the defunct Boston Children's Infirmary, which had failed more than 20 years before, according to one account because of "the deep-rooted and commendable feeling which prompts the mother to cling to her sick and suffering child, rather than entrust it to those whose motives she has never learned to fathom."

Started in 1869 as a 20-bed facility in a townhouse a short walk from Brown's home in the South End, Children's Hospital relocated to a larger building on the same street just one year later. Adeline Blanchard Tyler, an Episcopalian deaconess, was recruited to oversee daily operations. When illness prevented her continuing, she was succeeded by Sister Theresa and the Anglican Order of the Sisters of St. Margaret.

Most of the early patients were children whose parents were Irish immigrants. Many had traumatic injuries or infectious diseases, especially tuberculosis. Philanthropy completely supported the new institution. The Ladies' Aid Association provided essential supplies, including food, clothing, linens, towels, books, and toys. The success of the institution, with its careful combination of care and knowledge, led to the establishment of additional outpatient facilities and a convalescent home for the care of children outside Boston.

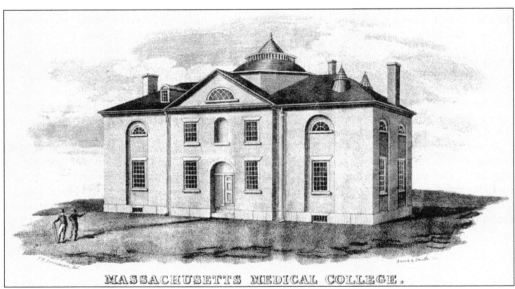

AMOS LAWRENCE: MERCHANT, INDUSTRIALIST, AND PHILANTHROPIST. The history of pediatric medicine in New England begins with Amos Lawrence, a textile magnate who helped usher in the Industrial Revolution with his mills along the Merrimack River in northeastern Massachusetts. After amassing his fortune from manufacturing cotton goods, Lawrence turned to philanthropy. Among his many ventures was the 1846 founding of the first children's infirmary in the nation. His son William, a physician who had recently graduated from Harvard Medical School, headed this new project.

THE CHILDREN'S INFIRMARY. Amos Lawrence purchased this building, which had been the site of Harvard Medical School since 1816, to house his proposed infirmary. His specific objective was to "secure the confidence of [the poor], and to overcome their repugnance to giving up their children to the care of others." He decided against this facility; instead, he purchased another building nearby on Washington Street. This infirmary never flourished, but it did admit 192 patients during its brief, 18-month existence. (Courtesy Harvard Medical Library.)

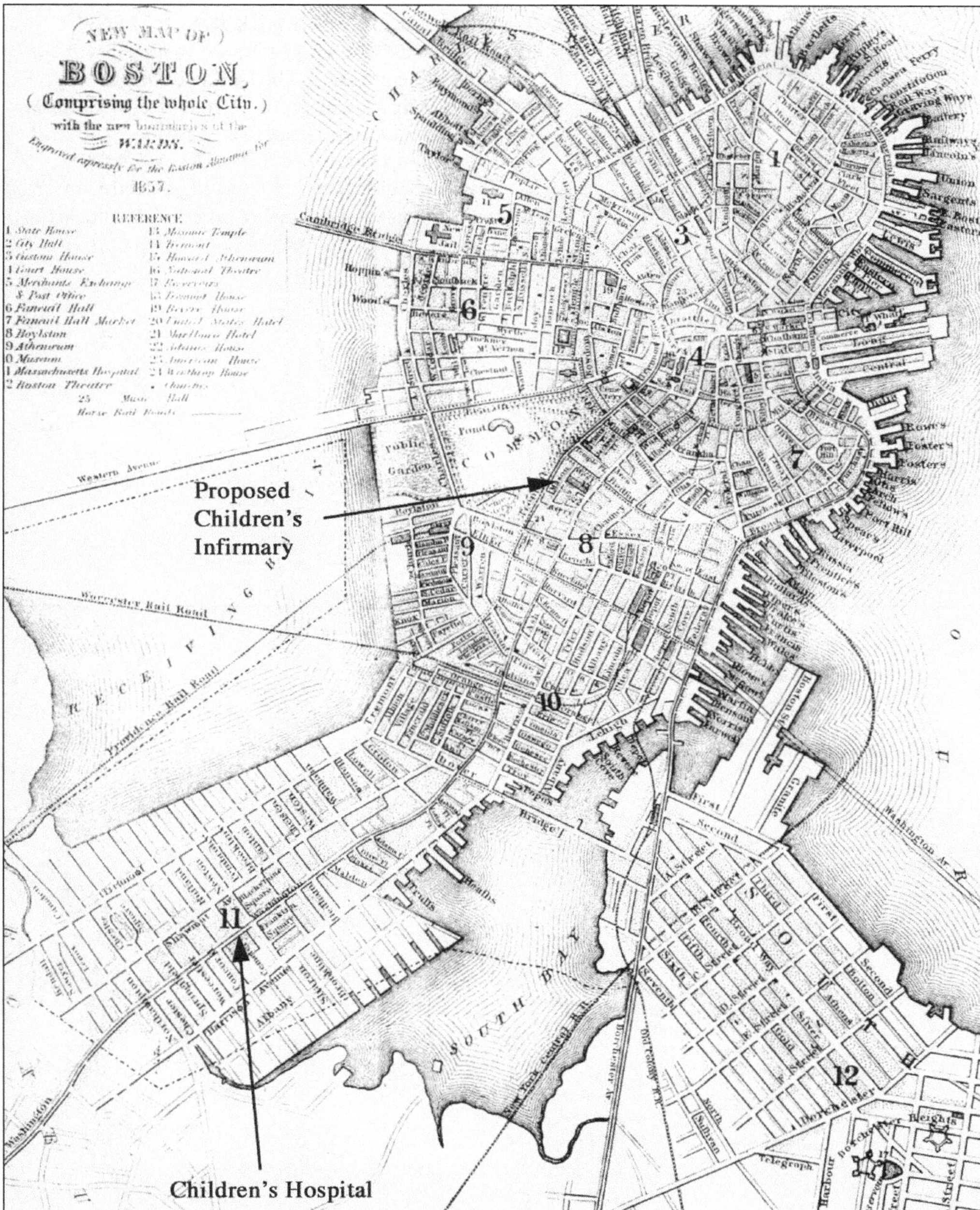

BOSTON LANDFILL, 1859. Amos Lawrence's attempt at creating a new hospital for the children of Boston's poor underscored the fact that the city was growing very quickly. Much of its growth was the result of the great influx of immigrants fleeing the Irish potato famine in the middle of the 19th century. This map illustrates how the small peninsula that was the original city of Boston began to expand in size with planned landfill. This southwestward expansion would include the site of the future Children's Hospital. Within 20 years, a new generation of young doctors realized it was time to reexamine Lawrence's idea for a children's hospital in Boston. (Printed in *The Boston Almanac*, 1859; courtesy Anthony Sammarco.)

DR. FRANCIS HENRY BROWN, C. 1869. Dr. Francis Brown graduated from Harvard Medical School in 1861 and served in the Civil War as a surgeon. When the war ended, Brown traveled throughout Europe, studying hospital architecture. Upon his return to Boston, he enlisted the aid of several former colleagues to start a new hospital for children.

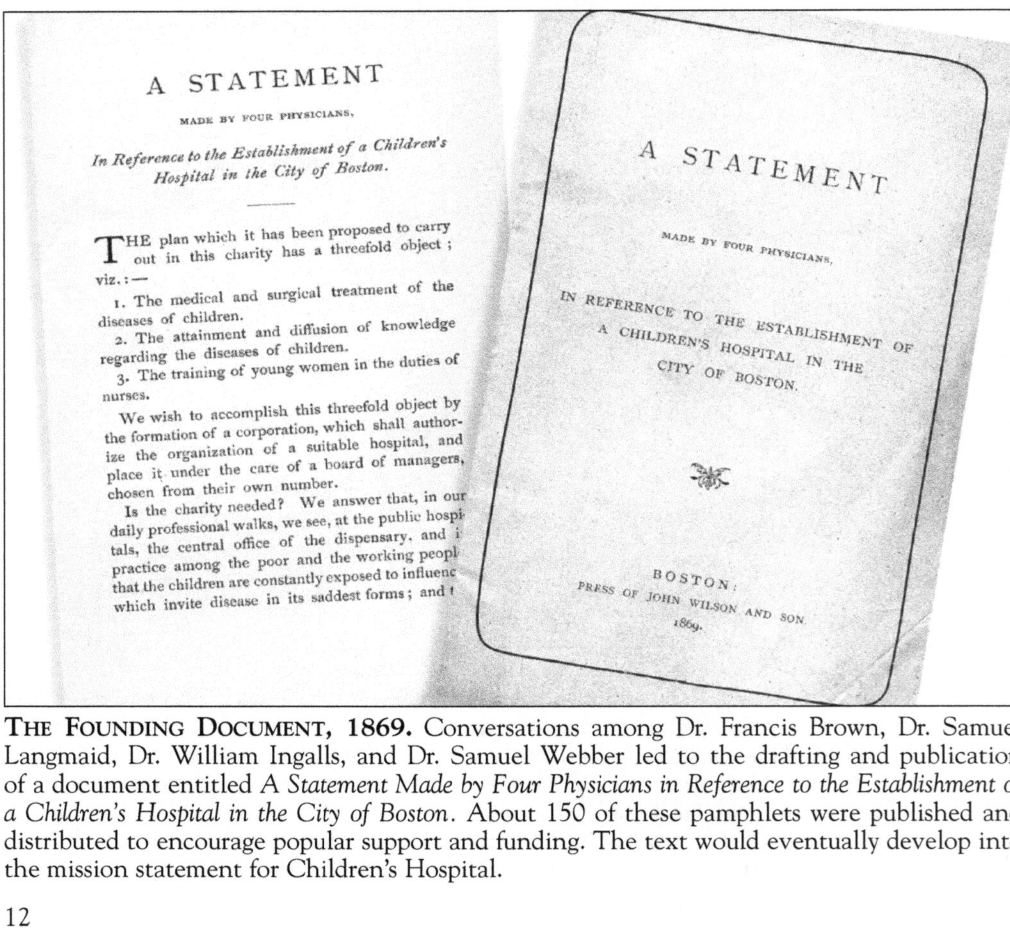

A STATEMENT

MADE BY FOUR PHYSICIANS,

In Reference to the Establishment of a Children's Hospital in the City of Boston.

THE plan which it has been proposed to carry out in this charity has a threefold object; viz.:—

1. The medical and surgical treatment of the diseases of children.
2. The attainment and diffusion of knowledge regarding the diseases of children.
3. The training of young women in the duties of nurses.

We wish to accomplish this threefold object by the formation of a corporation, which shall authorize the organization of a suitable hospital, and place it under the care of a board of managers, chosen from their own number.

Is the charity needed? We answer that, in our daily professional walks, we see, at the public hospitals, the central office of the dispensary, and i practice among the poor and the working peopl that the children are constantly exposed to influenc which invite disease in its saddest forms; and t

A STATEMENT

MADE BY FOUR PHYSICIANS,

IN REFERENCE TO THE ESTABLISHMENT OF A CHILDREN'S HOSPITAL IN THE CITY OF BOSTON.

BOSTON:
PRESS OF JOHN WILSON AND SON
1869.

THE FOUNDING DOCUMENT, 1869. Conversations among Dr. Francis Brown, Dr. Samuel Langmaid, Dr. William Ingalls, and Dr. Samuel Webber led to the drafting and publication of a document entitled *A Statement Made by Four Physicians in Reference to the Establishment of a Children's Hospital in the City of Boston*. About 150 of these pamphlets were published and distributed to encourage popular support and funding. The text would eventually develop into the mission statement for Children's Hospital.

ADELINE BLANCHARD TYLER. The hospital's founders knew they could not have a successful enterprise without the assistance of trained, compassionate nurses. Brown recruited Adeline Blanchard Tyler, a Billerica native who, after the death of her husband, had become an Episcopalian deaconess. Tyler agreed to move to Boston, where between 1869 and 1872 she served as superintendent of nurses.

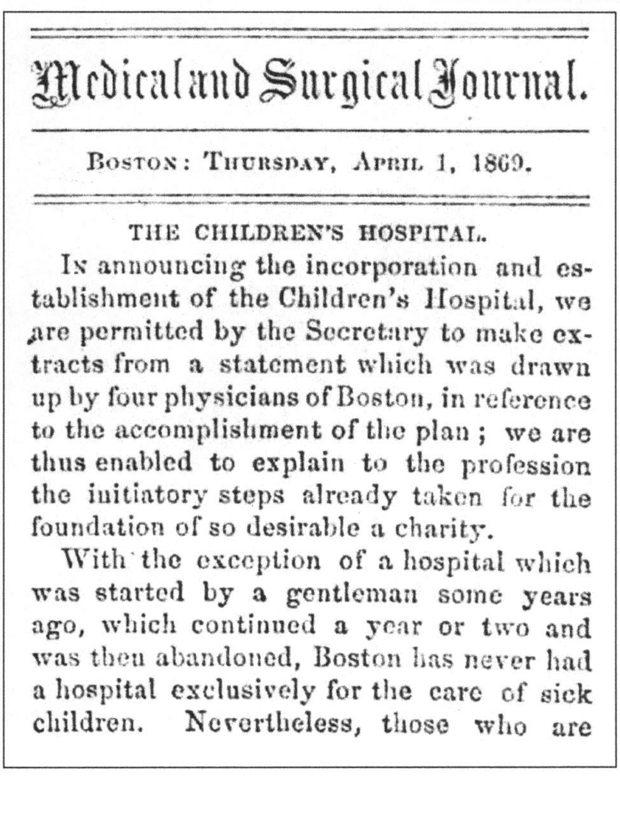

Medical and Surgical Journal.

BOSTON: THURSDAY, APRIL 1, 1869.

THE CHILDREN'S HOSPITAL.

IN announcing the incorporation and establishment of the Children's Hospital, we are permitted by the Secretary to make extracts from a statement which was drawn up by four physicians of Boston, in reference to the accomplishment of the plan; we are thus enabled to explain to the profession the initiatory steps already taken for the foundation of so desirable a charity.

With the exception of a hospital which was started by a gentleman some years ago, which continued a year or two and was then abandoned, Boston has never had a hospital exclusively for the care of sick children. Nevertheless, those who are

NOTICE OF THE FOUNDING, APRIL 1, 1869. This announcement appeared in the *Boston Medical and Surgical Journal* (now known as the *New England Journal of Medicine*): "In announcing the incorporation and establishment of the Children's Hospital, we are permitted by the Secretary to make extracts from a statement which was drawn up by four physicians of Boston, in reference to the accomplishment of the plan; we are thus enabled to explain to the profession the initiatory steps already taken for the foundation of so desirable a charity." (Courtesy Harvard Medical Library.)

CHILDREN'S HOSPITAL AT WASHINGTON AND RUTLAND STREETS, C. 1870. The appeal to the public was successful, and the physicians purchased a brick house on Rutland Street in Boston's South End, a 10-minute walk from Dr. Francis Brown's Waltham Street house. This marked the beginning of Children's Hospital. The impact of the little hospital (originally a 20-bed facility) on Boston's families was almost immediate, and within a year the managers of the hospital found it necessary to relocate to a larger building (shown here) on the corner of Washington and Rutland Streets. This building no longer exists; the space is now a public garden.

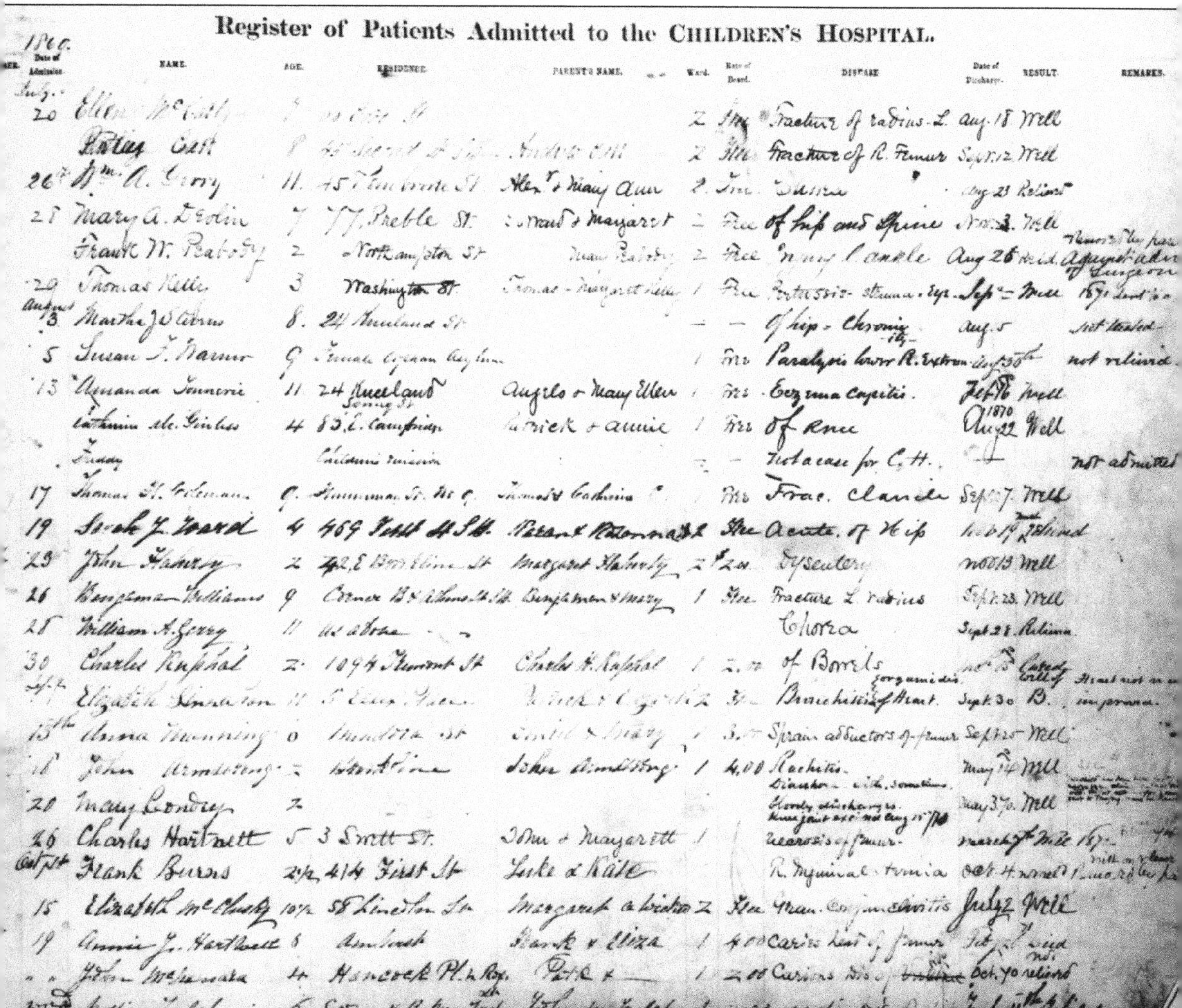

A REGISTER OF PATIENTS, 1869. The hospital's first admitted patient was Ellen McCarthy, a seven-year-old girl diagnosed with a fracture of the arm and discharged "well" after a stay of about a month. Many of the patients admitted to the hospital in these early years were treated for traumatic injuries and for conditions that were a consequence of tuberculosis. As a charitable institution, Children's Hospital did not usually charge families for care, nor did the attending physicians expect payment for their services. The hospital, like other pediatric institutions of that time, did not treat or admit infants under the age of two, eventually leading to the establishment of the Infants' Hospital years later.

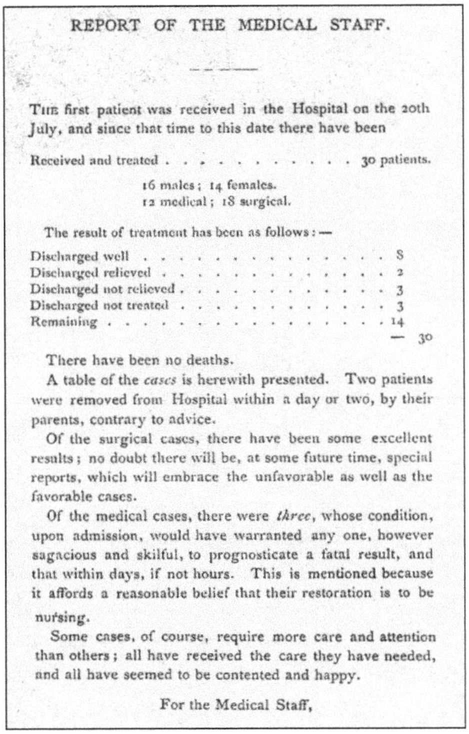

REPORT OF THE MEDICAL STAFF.

THE first patient was received in the Hospital on the 20th July, and since that time to this date there have been

Received and treated . . . . 30 patients.

16 males; 14 females.
12 medical; 18 surgical.

The result of treatment has been as follows: —

Discharged well	8
Discharged relieved	2
Discharged not relieved	3
Discharged not treated	3
Remaining	14
	— 30

There have been no deaths.

A table of the *cases* is herewith presented. Two patients were removed from Hospital within a day or two, by their parents, contrary to advice.

Of the surgical cases, there have been some excellent results; no doubt there will be, at some future time, special reports, which will embrace the unfavorable as well as the favorable cases.

Of the medical cases, there were *three*, whose condition, upon admission, would have warranted any one, however sagacious and skilful, to prognosticate a fatal result, and that within days, if not hours. This is mentioned because it affords a reasonable belief that their restoration is to be nursing.

Some cases, of course, require more care and attention than others; all have received the care they have needed, and all have seemed to be contented and happy.

For the Medical Staff,

A REPORT OF THE MEDICAL STAFF, DECEMBER 1869. The first annual report of Children's Hospital shows the early success of the institution. In the hospital's first five months, 30 patients were admitted, and the report notes that there were no deaths: "All have received the care they have needed, and all have seemed to be contented and happy."

THE SISTERS OF ST. MARGARET. The Sisters of St. Margaret succeeded Adeline Tyler in 1872, managing nursing care and training nursing staff for the next 45 years. Upon their arrival from England, they established a new convent in Boston's Louisburg Square (now the home of Sen. John F. Kerry). As many as eight sisters were on duty in the hospital at any one time; the services they rendered are memorialized in this plaque, now mounted in the lobby of the Hunnewell Building at Children's Hospital Boston.

THE

BOSTON MEDICAL AND SURGICAL JOURNAL.

New Series.] Thursday, November 17, 1870. [Vol. VI.—No. 20.

Original Communications.

A CASE OF PROGRESSIVE MUSCULAR SCLEROSIS, WITH A PAPER ON THE SAME.

By William Ingalls, M.D., one of the Physicians to The Children's Hospital, Boston, and S. G. Webber, M.D., Boston. Read before the Suffolk District Medical Society, Sept. 24th, 1870.

J. S., of Irish parentage, five years and two months old, was admitted into "The Children's Hospital" on the 2d September, 1870. To the age of three years he was quite a healthy child, but at about that period he began to move and act as though he had less strength than usual, and by degrees his mother came to acknowledge that such was really the case; this condition increased and the spinal column became very weak, and the "inward crook" of it was noticed by her.

Two weeks before admission he had a whitlow upon the fore-finger of his left hand, and one week before, he had a fall while attempting to run upon a sidewalk; from the first event the mother dated the special failing of his health, which she thought was increased by the second, and the evident decrease of his vital powers induced her to seek for him the benefits of the Hospital.

When first seen by the writer, the child was sitting in a corner of his bed, a soft pillow being behind him, he being in such a position that if a line had been carried from the end of the spine, over it, to the back of his head and continued on the same curve, it would have formed a circle, or nearly so.

On the day after admission, Dr. Webber saw the patient with me, and at once recognized the disease. We caused him to stand upon the floor, and he walked a few steps in a tottling or shambling manner. The spine presented a regular and exaggerated curve inward, from the third or fourth dorsal vertebra to the sacrum. This shape comes well under the name given by Duchenne—"saddle-back." A perfect picture of this child may be seen in Duchenne's book, éléctrisation localisée, 2nd edition, 1861, p. 355.

The head, while he was standing, and indeed while he was in any position which might have been called upright, gave to the spectator the idea that it was large and heavy, for the chin rested upon the sternum, and was inclined more to the right shoulder than to the left. A copy from Duchenne is presented.

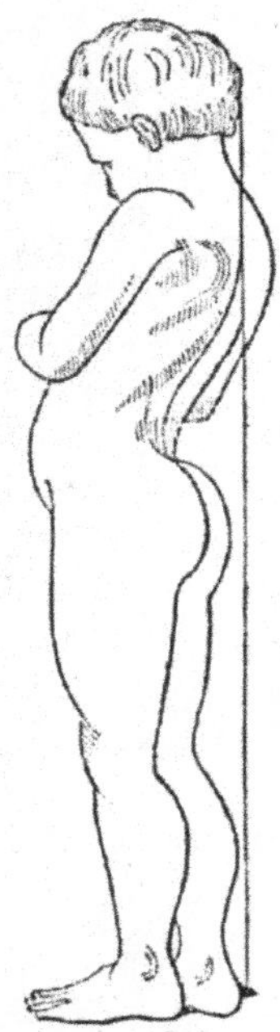

The muscles of the calves were largely developed, and the nates *seemed* to be so.

Upon attempting to take food, or even water, there was always a great choking and inability to swallow, so that it may be said he took no nourishment. He died on the fifth day after admission, having had convulsions on the day of his death. There was no post-mortem examination, but he undoubtedly died of pneumonia.

The want of precision and completeness in the history of this case is owing to the incapacity of the mother, and not to any want of diligence on the part of the interrogator; such as it is, it seems to introduce a valuable paper on the subject of the disease, by Dr. S. G. Webber.

The name placed at the commencement of this article is that used by Jaccoud, and is expressive of the change characteristic of this disease. Other names proposed are: progressive paralysis with apparent hypertrophy; pseudo-hypertrophic paralysis; progressive myosclerosis; and by Heller

An Early Children's Hospital Publication, November 17, 1870. From the beginning, the founders of Children's Hospital knew that to combat diseases and injuries of children in the future, the hospital needed to study the causes of these problems and promote scientific research. Dr. Francis Brown himself studied the importance of natural light and air quality in hospital architectural design, pioneered by Florence Nightingale, for enhancing patient treatment. Children's Hospital researchers have continued to tackle the most challenging medical problems and publish their work in prestigious medical journals. (Courtesy Harvard Medical Library.)

The Reception Room. This sketch from *Leslie's Illustrated Newspaper* of December 10, 1881, shows the receiving area of the hospital. Visible on the left is one of the Sisters of St. Margaret. Behind her, a mother and child sit in the waiting area.

A Patient Ward. Despite having already moved once, the hospital needed more space as early as the mid-1870s. Because patient wards were as crowded as the one shown here, managers began planning a larger facility. (Printed in *Leslie's Illustrated Newspaper*, December 10, 1881.)

Two

A Special Place for Children

Huntington Avenue, 1882–1914

After outgrowing the house they had attempted to use as a hospital, the managers (now called trustees) moved the facility west to Huntington Avenue, joining a number of other distinguished institutions that were taking advantage of the new land and fresh air away from the inner city. This larger building would be designed especially for children's needs. In it, Children's Hospital physicians and staff would pioneer new discoveries and integrate them with specialized care, create departments reflecting new diagnostic and therapeutic approaches, and accelerate the professionalization of pediatric physicians and nurses.

The dire needs of poor children had only increased, but so had society's unparalleled faith in scientific solutions. In 1890, Jacob Riis had documented "How the Other Half Lives" in New York City. By 1912, a textile strike in Lawrence (named for the family who had started the Children's Infirmary) and similar events around the nation would draw attention to miserable factory conditions. Yet even William Jennings Bryan, populist champion, could write in 1911 of the "unending struggle upward, with no limit to human advancement or development." This era led to the creation and pervasive assimilation of progressive ideals that fit exactly the organized, scientific approach to medicine, the spirit of inquiry, and dedication that inspired Children's Hospital clinical and research staff and leadership.

The beginning of this period has been described as "the dark age of pediatrics with a few strokes of dawn just beginning to lighten the sky." In 1910, Abraham Flexner released a report stating that only one medical school in 155 provided acceptable education. During this same era, however, the practice of pediatrics was recognized as a specialty, and the first appointment was made to the Harvard Medical School faculty of a physician devoted solely to the care of children. In 1895, Wilhelm Roentgen discovered x-rays (a major diagnostic advance), and other discoveries rapidly followed. Although the hospital staff continued to treat primarily orthopedic problems largely resulting from tuberculosis, several new fields devoted to pediatric diseases evolved, including radiology, dentistry, neurology, pathology, and laryngology.

As the range of hospital care expanded, so did the need to train specially qualified staff. During this time, the first medical "house officers" (young physicians who were called "internes" and "externes") were appointed. A nursing school also opened to educate additional nurses to join what some saw as the "best nurses in the world."

CHILDREN'S HOSPITAL AT HUNTINGTON AVENUE, C. 1882. By the end of 1880, a capital campaign had raised $95,000, and plans were announced to build a larger facility on the north side of Huntington Avenue. The new hospital, designed specifically for the care of children, opened on December 26, 1882, and provided beds for 60 patients. An additional wing with 36 beds opened in 1890.

HUNTINGTON AVENUE, IN FRONT OF CHILDREN'S HOSPITAL, C. 1905. The hospital's move to Huntington Avenue marked the beginning of a movement westward of several prominent Boston institutions following the Great Boston Fire of 1872. Within 25 years, the barren landscape around Children's Hospital was transformed into a bustling cultural center on what would be called the "Avenue of the Arts." In this photograph, a hospital physician departs from a recently launched streetcar on Huntington Avenue, and several nurses board. Symphony Hall is visible to the right of the hospital.

BOSTON BASEBALL BEFORE FENWAY PARK, 1903. The Boston American League baseball club (officially named the Boston Red Sox in 1907) made its home at the Huntington Avenue Grounds, on what is now the site of Northeastern University. Baseball games were visible from the uppermost windows of Children's Hospital. In 1903, Boston defeated the National League champion Pittsburgh Pirates to win the first official World Series ever played. The Red Sox moved to the new Fenway Park (named for the Fens area in Boston's Back Bay) in 1912. (Courtesy Boston Public Library.)

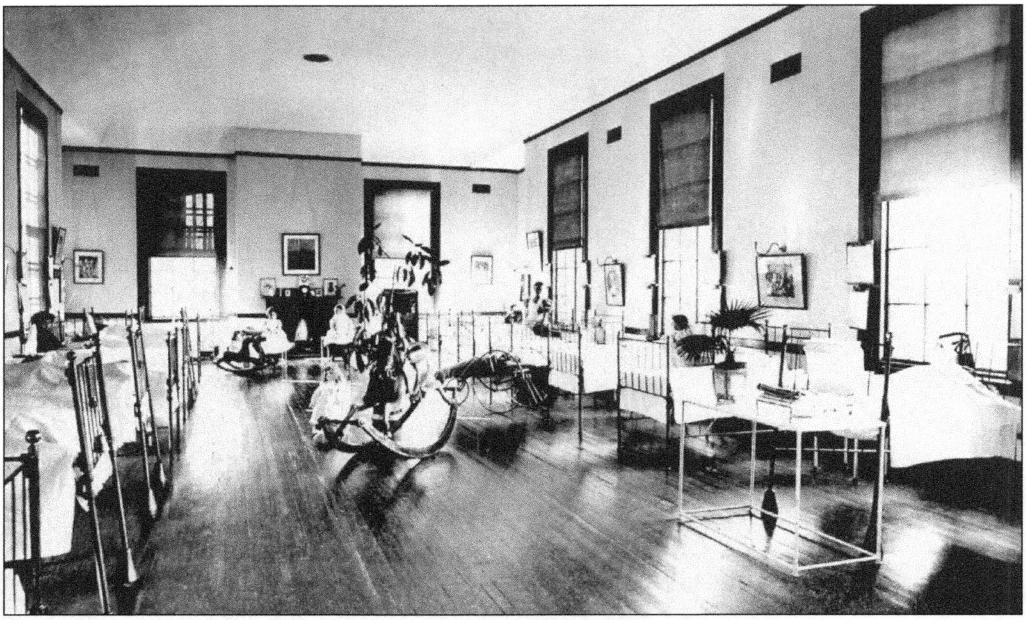

The Girls' Surgical Ward. Dr. Francis Brown's studies of hospital design and hygiene reflected the belief at the time that the best conditions for patients included plenty of natural light and fresh air. Accordingly, the new hospital building contained wards with high ceilings and many windows to provide ventilation and fireplaces for heat.

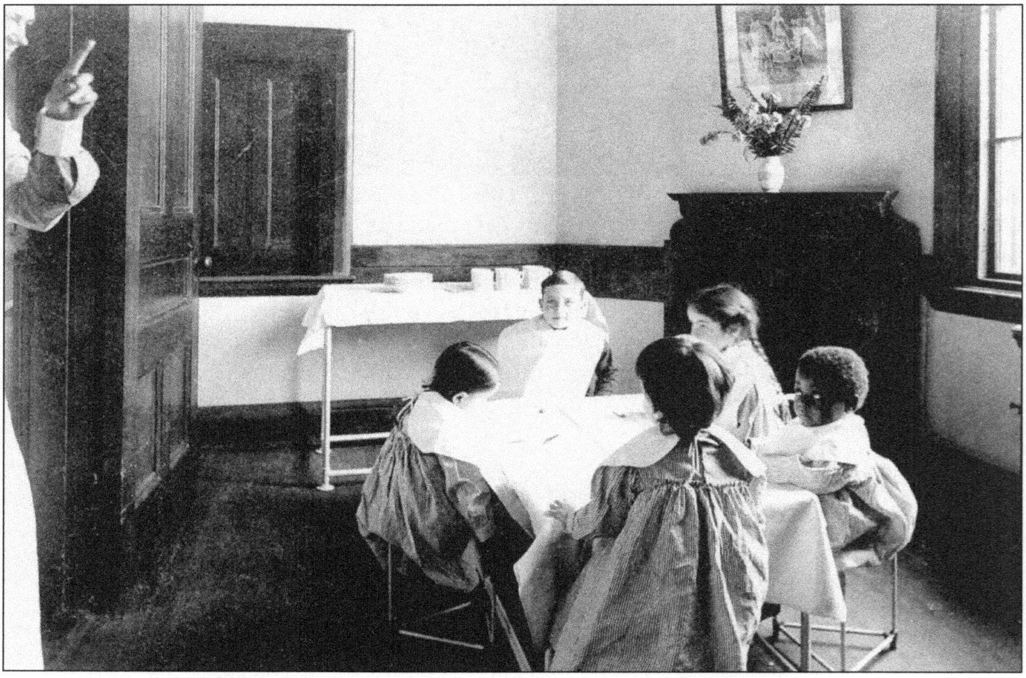

Early "Meals on Wheels," c. 1900. Ambulatory or portable dining for patients was provided. Many children were unable to walk because of a variety of problems, and it was more practical to deliver meals directly to the patients.

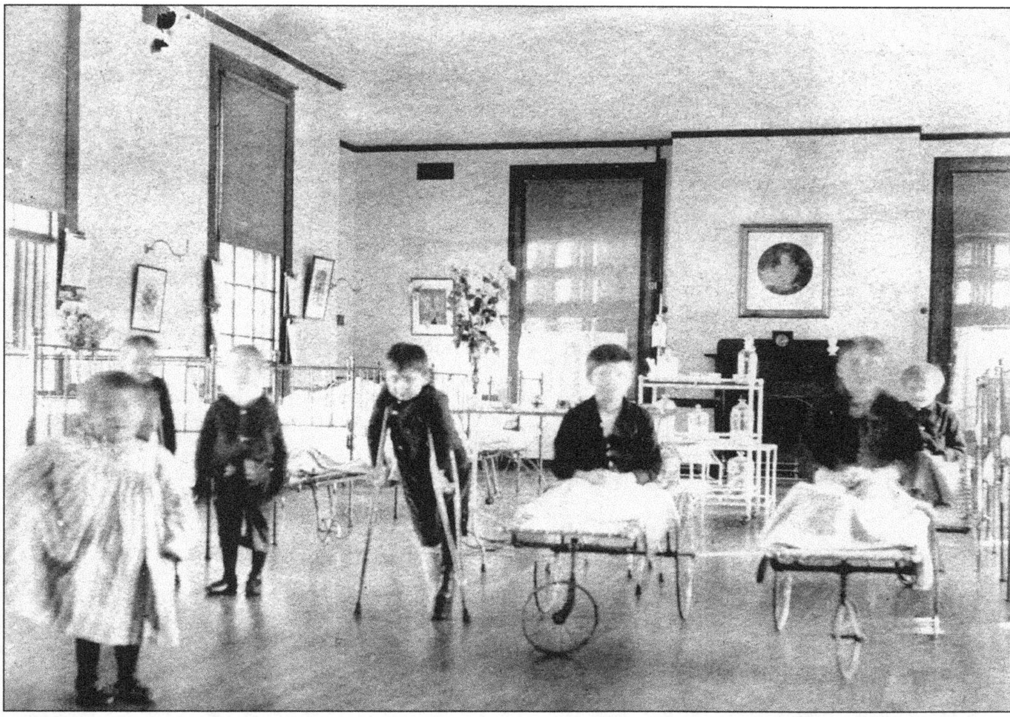

PATIENTS IN THE BOYS' WARD, C. 1910. Children's Hospital grew rapidly and treated a wide variety of illnesses and injuries. Two-thirds of the patients admitted between 1882 and 1914 were treated for complications of tuberculosis. In these photographs, several children are in carts or on crutches, suggestive of cases of orthopedic tuberculosis.

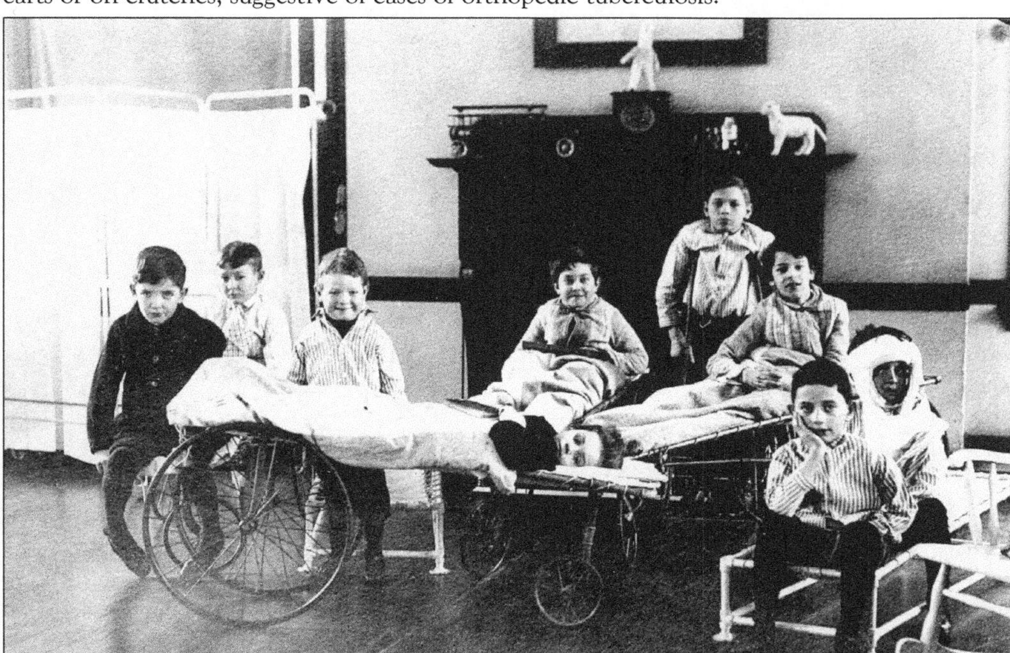

Dr. Thomas Morgan Rotch. A major figure in the early history of Children's Hospital, Dr. Thomas Morgan Rotch was physician in chief from 1893 until his death in 1914. He was also appointed medical director of the Infants' Hospital in 1899 and chairman of the newly created Department of Pediatrics at Harvard Medical School in 1903. Rotch's 1,100-page textbook, *Pediatrics: The Hygiene and Medical Treatment of Children* (1895), a testament to his knowledge and dedication, was the standard pediatric reference of the time.

Nurses Preparing Milk, c. 1910. Milk from infected cows was soon recognized as a common source of disease, especially among poor children. Dr. Thomas Morgan Rotch and his colleagues believed that they could improve the milk supply scientifically. In 1891, Rotch established a milk laboratory for research and clinical use. The importance of laboratory study was immediately recognized.

DR. EDWARD H. BRADFORD: COMBATING TUBERCULOSIS. Dr. Edward H. Bradford was one of Children's Hospital's leading surgeons and a pioneer in the treatment of orthopedic tuberculosis. A member of the hospital staff from 1878 to 1912, Bradford served as dean of Harvard Medical School from 1912 to 1918. In 1890, he wrote a 780-page orthopedic textbook that became the standard. He was a founder of the American Orthopedic Association and the Industrial School for Crippled Children, still in existence as the Cotting School. (Courtesy Harvard University Portrait Collection.)

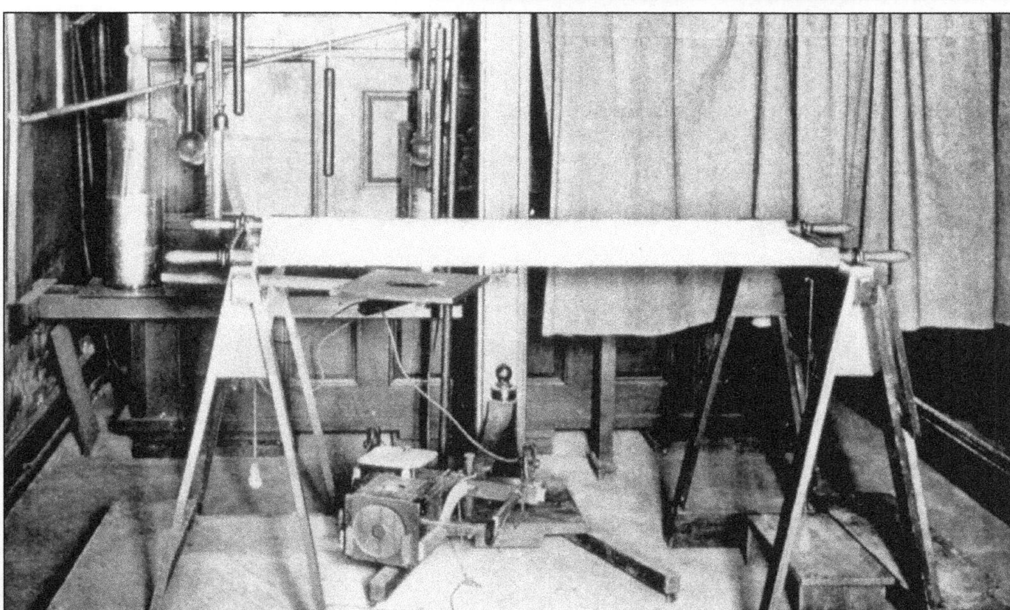

ROENTGEN RAYS AND RADIOLOGY. Shortly after Wilhelm Roentgen discovered x-rays in 1895, physicians at Children's Hospital put the new technology to good use. Dr. Ernest Codman was appointed the first hospital skiagrapher (x-ray expert); when Codman produced glass-plate "roentgenograms" in 1899, pediatric radiology began. This photograph shows early radiology equipment similar to that used at Children's Hospital.

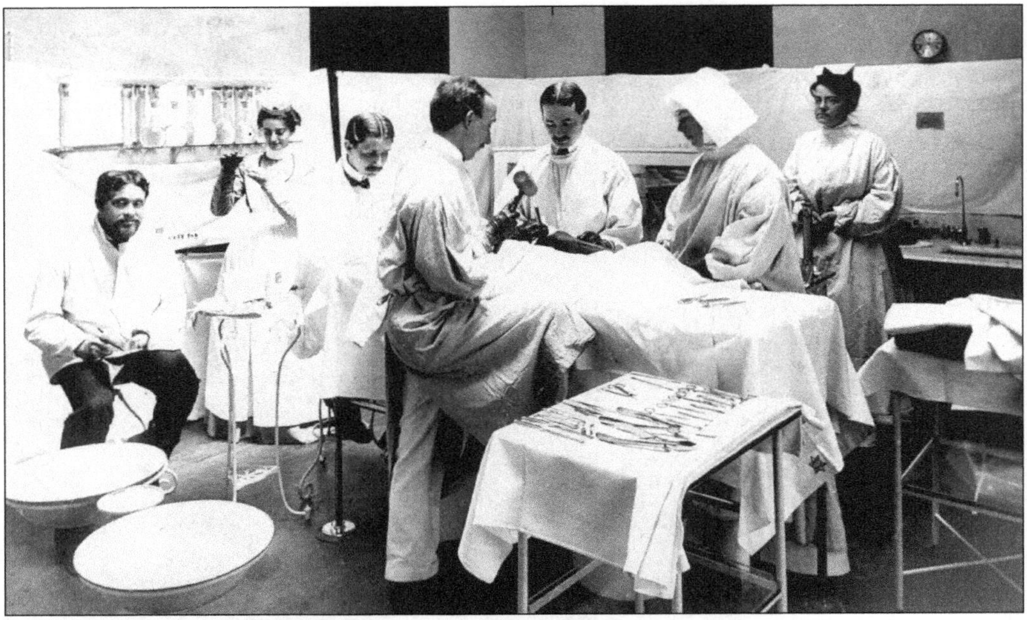

An Operating Room, c. 1900. As knowledge increased and new technologies such as anesthesia, antisepsis, and x-rays grew in use, surgical procedures greatly advanced. In the early 1900s, Children's Hospital separated surgery and orthopedics into two distinct departments. Note the absence of caps and masks in this early period.

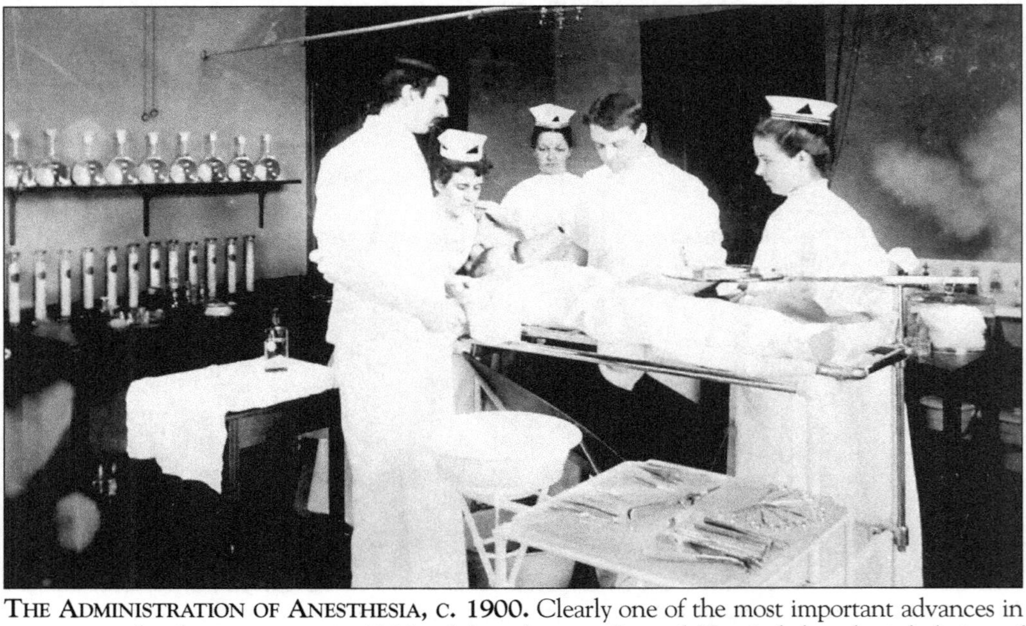

The Administration of Anesthesia, c. 1900. Clearly one of the most important advances in surgery was the demonstration in 1846 at Massachusetts General Hospital that the inhalation of ether could make surgery pain-free. Subsequently, surgeons did not have to rush through procedures and could operate on previously untreatable surgical conditions. Anesthesia was usually administered in the operating room by a nurse, medical student, or young surgical resident.

AN OUTPATIENT CHECKUP, c. 1910. Many illnesses did not warrant admission to the hospital. In 1875, Children's Hospital initially rented a building near the Washington and Rutland location to serve as its outpatient clinic. When the Huntington Avenue building opened in 1882, 421 patients visited the new outpatient clinic. By 1889, nearly 6,000 patients were treated annually in this outpatient setting.

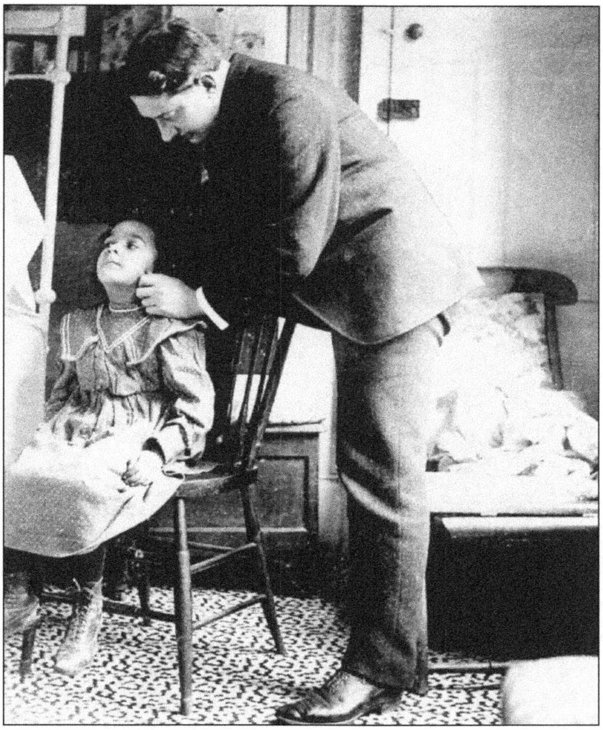

DR. SAMUEL LANGMAID, c. 1890. One of the four founding fathers of Children's Hospital, Dr. Samuel Langmaid went on to become the institution's first chief of "diseases of the throat." This was the beginning of what is now the Department of Otolaryngology, currently at the forefront of care for children with hearing, speech, and airway problems. (Courtesy Harvard Medical Library.)

A DOCTORS' ROOM, C. 1910. Staff physicians and medical students benefitted from a place to take a brief break or discuss cases with their colleagues, away from the bustle of the rest of the hospital. Early in its history, Children's Hospital developed a strong program of support for its medical and nursing staffs.

THE NURSES' HOUSE ON GAINSBOROUGH STREET, C. 1910. The Sisters of St. Margaret and the nurses of Children's Hospital were essential to the success of the hospital. With the institution's relocation to Huntington Avenue in 1882, nurses moved into quarters opposite the hospital on Gainsborough Street. They worked around the clock in 12-hour shifts until 1896, when the hospital adopted an eight-hour workday. Because of the great demand for outpatient services, nurses and physicians also made visits to patients' homes. This program was called the Out-Door Relief Department, which eventually developed into the hospital's Social Service Department.

SISTER SUSANNA AS A NOVICE AT CHILDREN'S HOSPITAL, C. 1890. The Sisters of St. Margaret served as teachers, caregivers, and supervisors. In this photograph, Sister Susanna reads to a child. An 1893 graduate of the training school, she eventually became Mother Susanna of the Convent of St. Margaret and served as superintendent of Children's Hospital from 1908 to 1912. The superintendent admitted patients, ordered medical supplies, kept patient records, responded to letters of inquiry about the hospital and training school, recorded all donations, received visitors, gave tours of the hospital building, engaged and dismissed nurses and support employees, and sent monthly reports to the board of managers.

The School of Nursing Graduating Class of 1896. The Sisters established a School of Nursing at Children's Hospital in 1889 to ensure a steady supply of nurses, not only for Children's Hospital but also for other medical institutions in Boston and beyond. Originally, the school offered a two-year program for young women; in 1895, it became a three-year program.

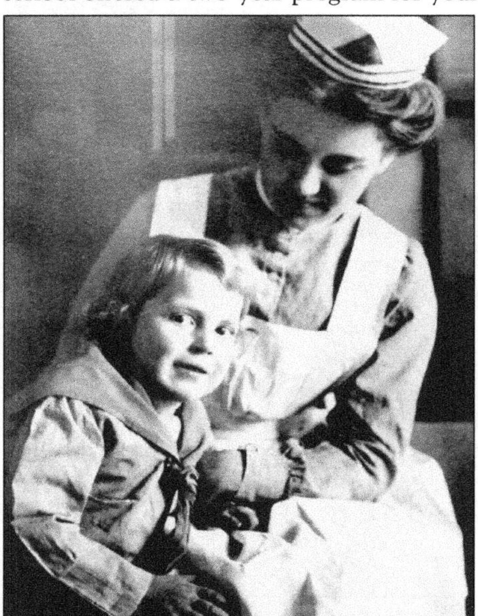

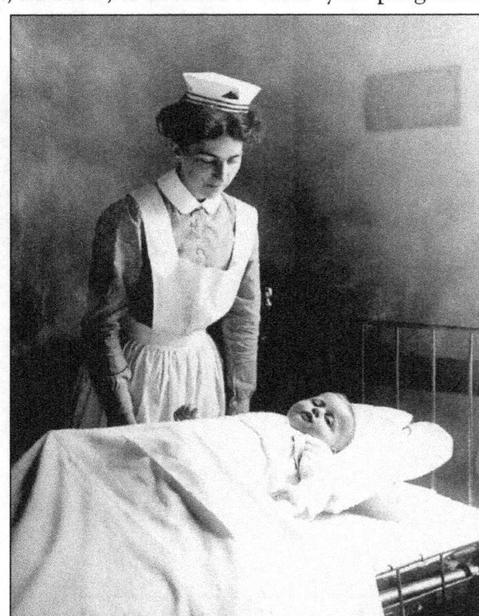

Nurses Caring for Young Children, c. 1900. Students of the nursing school staffed several hospitals and treatment facilities for children, including the Infants' Hospital, then on Blossom Street in Boston, and the Wellesley Convalescent Home, a long-term care facility for children disabled by diseases such as tuberculosis, polio, and rickets. The nurses' distinctive "strawberry box" caps had narrow bands that reflected the number of years of education, with one wide band replacing three narrow bands upon graduation.

CHILDREN'S HOSPITAL PATIENTS, C. 1895. In this turn-of-the-century photograph, many toys are evident. Gifts were donated by numerous volunteers and charitable organizations such as the Children's Mission and the Ladies' Aid Association. Their efforts helped make the lives of patients as comfortable as possible.

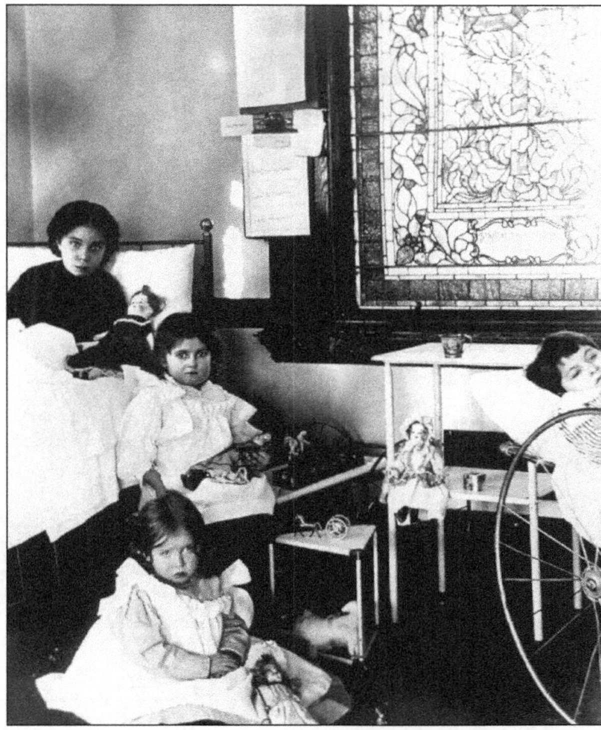

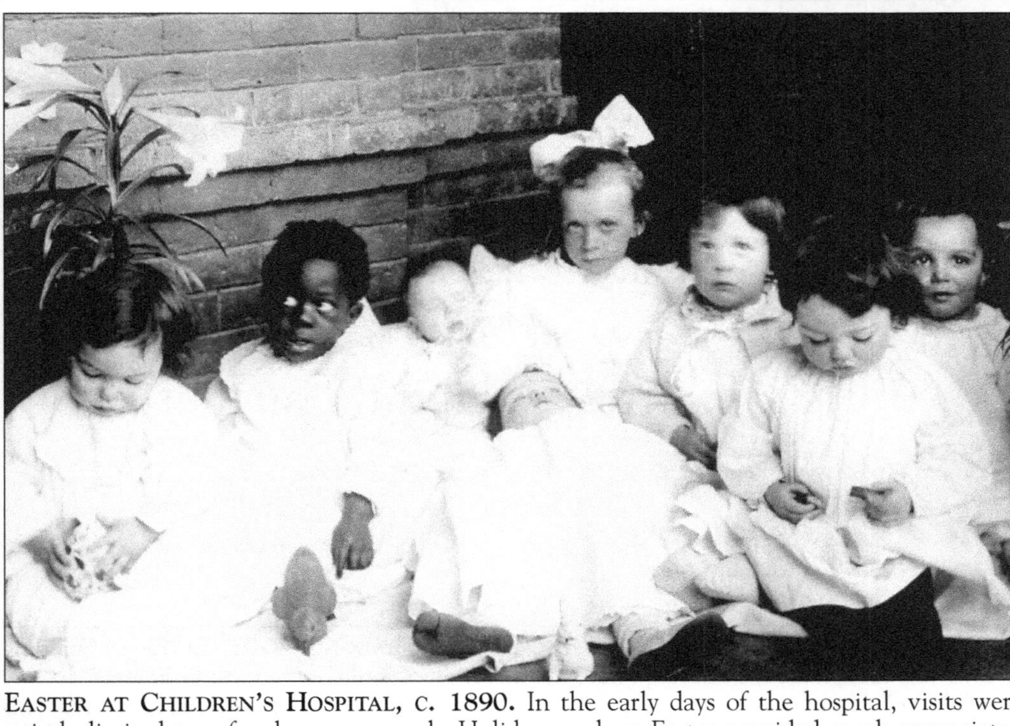

EASTER AT CHILDREN'S HOSPITAL, C. 1890. In the early days of the hospital, visits were strictly limited to a few hours per week. Holidays such as Easter provided much-appreciated opportunities for celebration.

HOUSE OFFICERS, 1902. The hospital began a program of practical education for medical students, many of whom were from Harvard Medical School. Concurrent with the move to Huntington Avenue in 1882, house officers were first appointed as "internes" and "externes." By 1914, six house officers were in training for six-month appointments. They assisted the medical and surgical staff in a variety of activities.

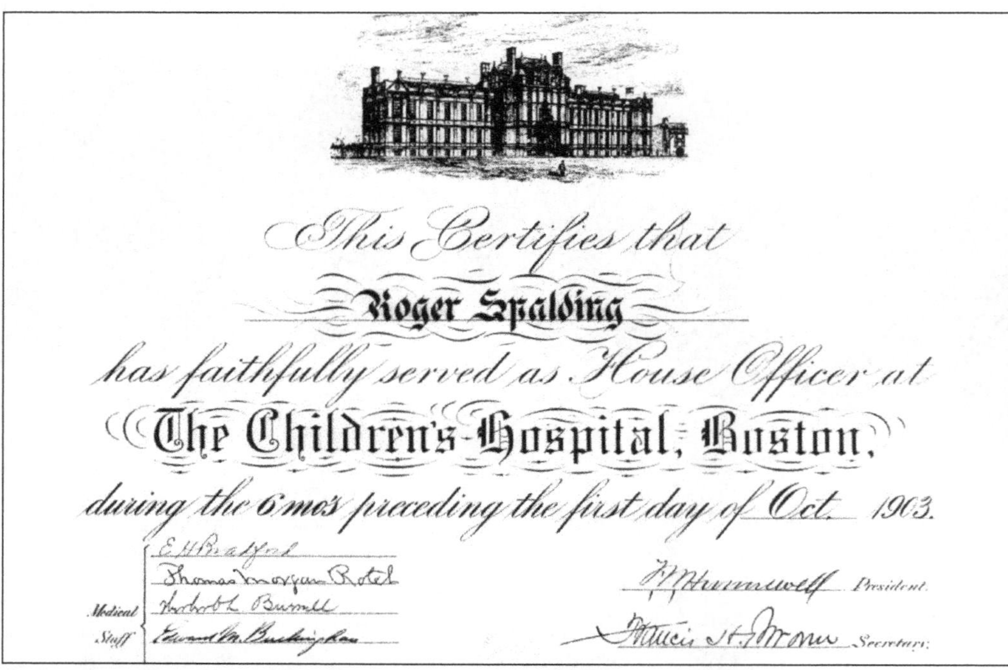

This Certifies that

Roger Spalding

has faithfully served as House Officer at

The Children's Hospital, Boston,

during the 6 mo's preceding the first day of Oct. 1903.

Medical Staff: E H Bradford; Thomas Morgan Rotch; Herbert L. Burrell; Edward M. Buckingham

President.

Secretary.

A CERTIFICATE OF COMPLETION OF HOUSE OFFICER TRAINING, 1903. Dr. Roger Spalding successfully completed his training under the direction of some of the most prominent doctors at Children's Hospital, including Dr. Edward Bradford and Dr. Thomas Morgan Rotch. This certificate indicates that Brown still served the hospital as its secretary in 1903, a position he held for more than 30 years.

THE APOTHECARY SHOP, C. 1910. Children's Hospital offered auxiliary services to provide medicines and other types of treatment. Shown here is the hospital's apothecary, or pharmacy.

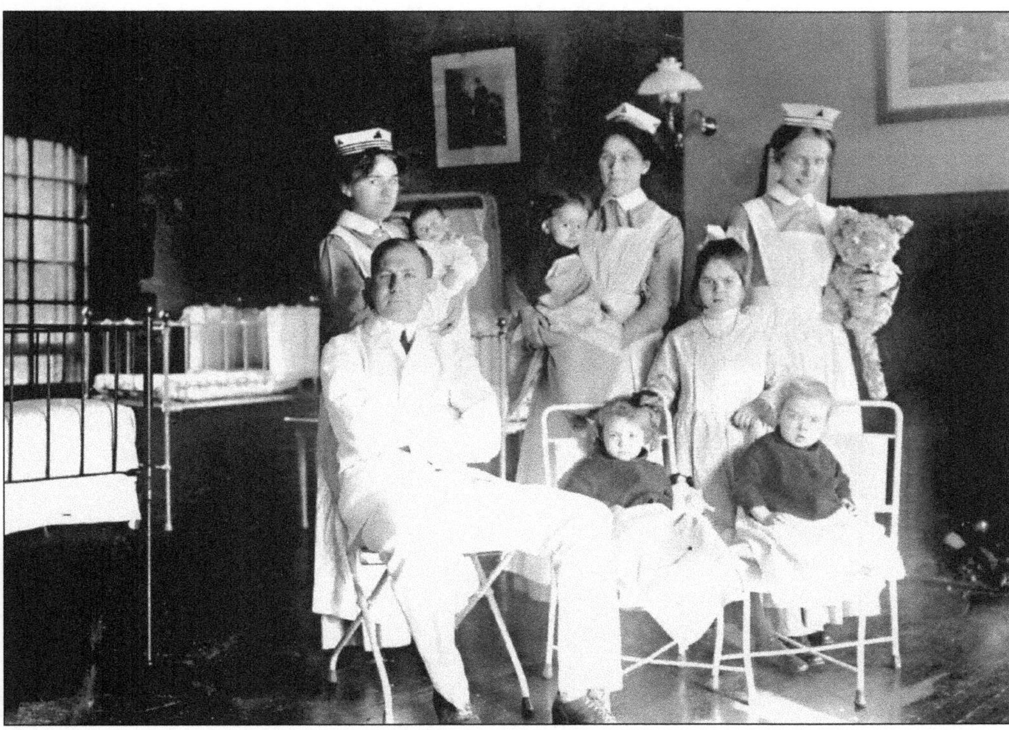

A DOCTOR WITH NURSES AND PATIENTS, C. 1905. This scene in the girls' ward shows a physician with three nurses and five patients (and one teddy bear, a Teddy Roosevelt namesake of that era). The photograph conveys the pride the doctors and nurses took in their professional work and the personal concern they had for their patients.

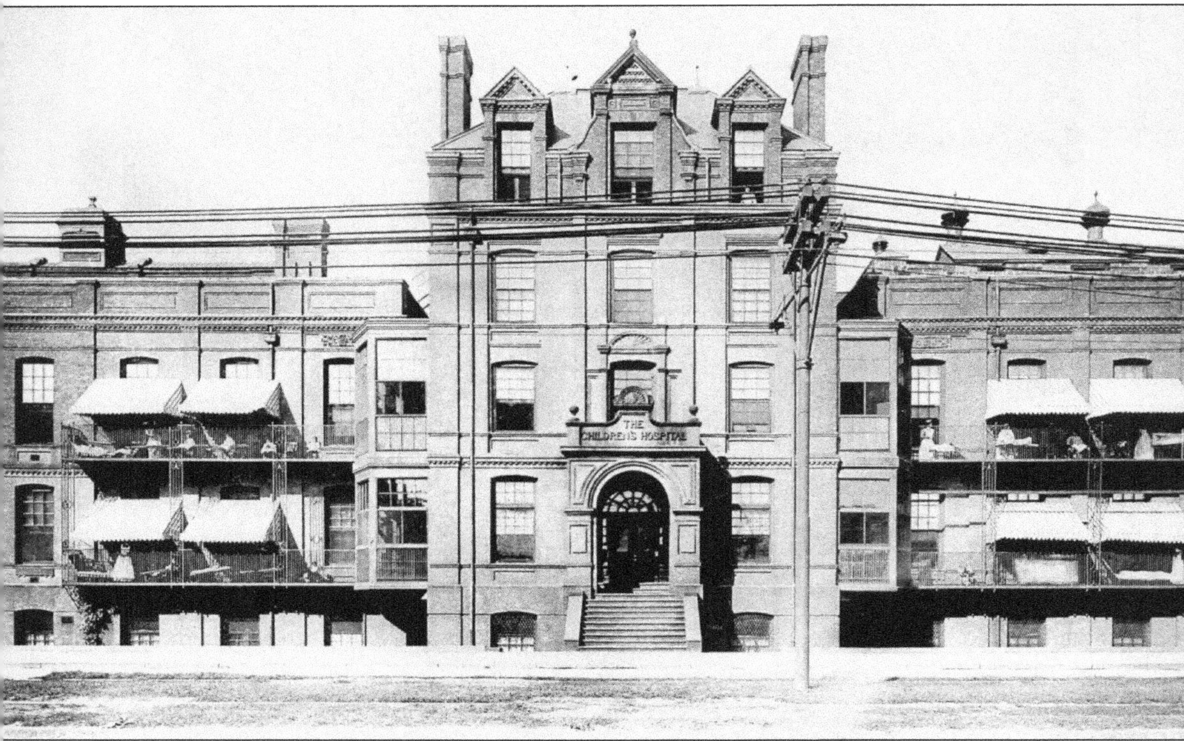

CHILDREN'S HOSPITAL, 1913. Nurses and patients relax on the sun porches installed during the final years on Huntington Avenue. Contemporary practice emphasized the benefits of fresh air and sunlight for the treatment of rickets, tuberculosis, and a variety of infectious diseases. Children's Hospital stood on the threshold of the modern era of medicine and would soon become an internationally recognized leader. The site where the Huntington Avenue building was once located is now a row of retail shops and restaurants adjacent to Symphony Hall.

Three

FERTILE GROUND

LONGWOOD AVENUE, 1914–1946

Within 30 years of the move to the new hospital on Huntington Avenue, it became clear that a larger, updated facility was required to meet patients' needs. In addition, the hospital's leadership understood that a closer association with Harvard Medical School would foster major scientific advances. When the school relocated to a new site on Longwood Avenue, Children's Hospital moved adjacent, to a $120,000, three-acre site on the former Ebenezer Francis farm, where "the air was purer and the noise and jar less." The mutually fruitful relationship with Harvard and the opening of a new nursing school helped Children's Hospital move to the forefront of pediatric discovery, patient treatment, and medical education. Outstanding medical research, clinical advances, and exemplary teaching were integrated with the best possible environment for care.

In the turbulent decades between 1914 and 1946, the hospital's growing preeminence paralleled many important advances in the world of medicine. In 1929, Alexander Fleming reported on the singular effects of the *penicillium* fungus, and by the early 1940s—in time for the next great war—penicillin was in manufacture. Using sulfa and other antimicrobials like streptomycin, physicians had new weapons—and new credibility—in fighting infectious diseases. Among other notable discoveries, the 1930s also brought the electron microscope, the promise of understanding the structure of viruses, the discovery of blood factors, and the development of heroic innovations in surgery.

During this era, new discoveries were reflected in further changes in the organization and structure of Children's Hospital. Visionary academic and clinical leaders emerged within medicine and surgery. Research laboratories opened. Cystic fibrosis, *erythroblastosis fetalis*, and many other childhood diseases were described and studied. Medicine began to sub-specialize into metabolism, hematology, and bacteriology. Scientist-physicians developed new methods of understanding and maintaining the chemical structure of the body's fluids, which improved the treatment of diarrheal diseases. Children's Hospital surgeons perfected new techniques for repairing congenital abnormalities and initiated the field of cardiac surgery. Major advances occurred in neurology relating to birth injuries, cerebral palsy, and lead poisoning. The iron lung was developed by scientists at the nearby Harvard School of Public Health and put into practice at Children's Hospital, together with various forms of hydrotherapy and physiotherapy, to treat victims of polio epidemics.

Harvard medical students also began learning pediatrics on the hospital's new campus. Residency, the period of postgraduate clinical training of new physicians, grew from four trainees in 1900 to more than 30 in the early 1940s. A formal curriculum replaced apprenticeship for interns and residents. Women became residents when male physicians left to serve in World War II.

Philanthropy and volunteerism continued as essential contributors to Children's Hospital's success but also assumed a more organized form through the Medical Alumni Association, the Children's Hospital Birthday Club, the Ladies' Aid Association, and the Welfare Committee.

These changes provided Children's Hospital with a strong foundation for growth and success in the ensuing years.

CLEAN COUNTRY AIR. After Children's Hospital opened on Huntington Avenue in 1882, the expansion of Boston continued to the Fens area and Longwood Avenue on the border of Brookline. Several institutions relocated here, but the most prominent was Harvard Medical School in 1906. Children's Hospital followed in 1914. This 1903 photograph shows the location of the future medical school and Children's Hospital at the site of the old Francis farm.

THE HARVARD MEDICAL SCHOOL AREA, 1921. Here, Harvard Medical School is located in the center. The new Children's Hospital is the domed building on the left, with the new Infants' Hospital below it. In the foreground, the Peter Bent Brigham Hospital appears below the medical school.

FRANCIS WELLES HUNNEWELL. Francis Hunnewell (1838–1917) was a successful real-estate developer in the Allston-Brighton neighborhoods of Boston during the mid- to late 19th century. A resident of Cleveland Circle, he made major donations to Children's Hospital during the Huntington years, and the new hospital building on Longwood Avenue was named in his honor. It continues to bear his family name.

The New Children's Hospital, 1914. The Hunnewell Building, the oldest continuously occupied structure at Children's Hospital, originally contained 145 beds. The central section of the building held reception and examining rooms, the X-Ray Department, and a variety of administrative quarters. The west wing (right) contained the hospital's dispensary, a receiving room, waiting areas, examining and treatment rooms for all medical and surgical departments, plaster rooms, and the gymnasium. At the top of the dispensary, a special ward was dedicated to private or isolation patients. Seventy nurses lived in the eastern side of the building (left). In addition, it contained five rooms for the Sisters of St. Margaret. The steeple shown in this architectural proposal was never erected; a dome was built instead.

Children's Hospital, 1919. In front of the Hunnewell Building, specially bred cows graze. They provided safe, tuberculosis-free milk for patients at both the Children's and Infants' Hospitals.

The Hunnewell Building, c. 1920. Next to Children's Hospital stood row houses where physicians in training resided. The site is now occupied by the Enders Research Building.

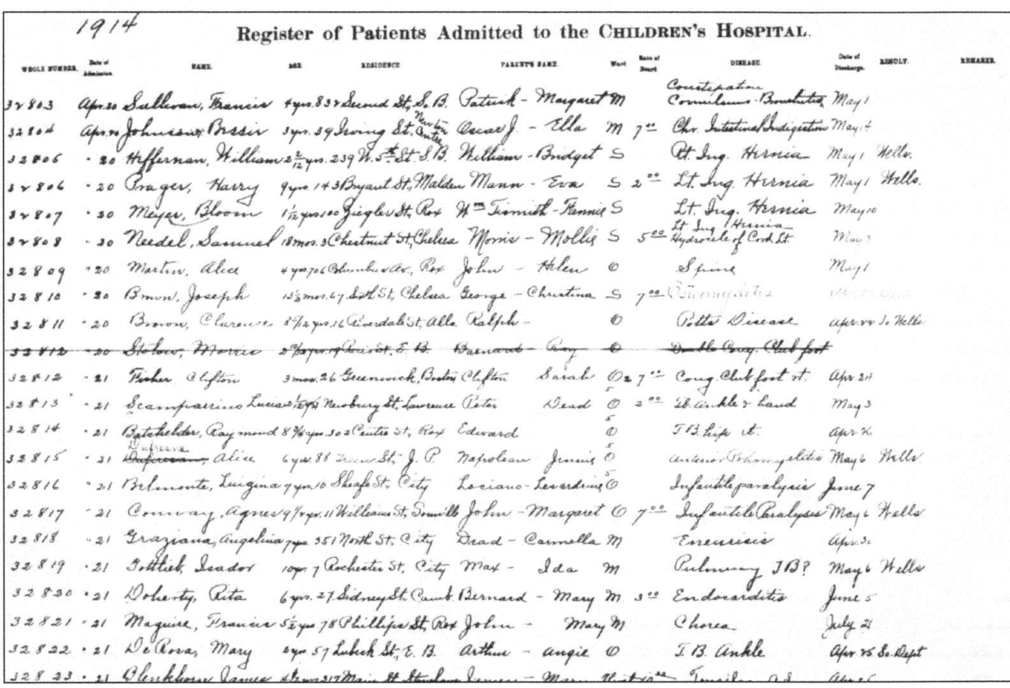

1914

Register of Patients Admitted to the Children's Hospital.

Whole Number	Date of Admission	Name	Age	Residence	Parent's Name	Ward	Date of Board	Disease	Date of Discharge	Result	Remarks
32803	Apr. 20	Sullivan, Francis	4 yrs.	83 Second St, S.B.	Patrick - Margaret	M		Constipation Convulsions Bronchitis	May 1		
32804	Apr. 20	Johnson, Bessie	3 yrs.	39 Irving St. Newton Centre	Oscar J. - Ella	M	7	Chr. Intestinal Indigestion	May 14		
32805	20	Heffernan, William	2 2/12 yrs.	239 W. 5th St. S.B.	William - Bridget	S		Rt. Ing. Hernia	May 1	Well	
32806	20	Prager, Harry	9 yrs.	143 Bryant St, Malden	Mann - Eva	S	2	Lt. Ing. Hernia	May 1	Well	
32807	20	Meyer, Bloom	1 1/2 yrs.	100 Ziegler St. Rox	Wm Trimith - Fannie	S		Lt. Ing. Hernia	May 10		
32808	20	Needel, Samuel	18 mos.	3 Chestnut St, Chelsea	Morris - Mollie	S	5	Lt. Ing. Hernia Hydrocele of Cord Lt.	May		
32809	20	Martin, Alice	4 yrs.	706 Columbus Av., Rox	John - Helen	O		Spine	May 1		
32810	20	Brown, Joseph	15 1/2 mos.	67 Sixth St, Chelsea	George - Christina	S	7	[illegible]			
32811	20	Brown, Clarence	8 1/2 yrs.	16 Riverdale St, Alls.	Ralph -	O		Pott's Disease	Apr.		Well
~~32812~~	~~20~~	~~Stolow, Morris~~	~~2 1/2 yrs.~~	~~[illegible] St. E.B.~~	~~Barnard - Rosy~~	~~O~~		~~Double Cong. Club foot~~			
32812	21	Fisher, Clifton	3 mos.	26 Greenwich, Boston	Clifton - Sarah	O	7	Cong. Club foot rt.	Apr 24		
32813	21	Scampariino Lucia	5 yrs.	Newbury St, Lawrence	Peter - Dead	O	2	Lt. Ankle & hand	May 3		
32814	21	Batchelder, Raymond	8 3/4 yrs.	302 Centre St, Rox	Edward	O		T.B. hip rt.	Apr		
32815	21	Dufresne, Alice	6 yrs.	88 [illegible] St. J.P.	Napoleon - Jennie	O		Anterior Poliomyelitis	May 6	Well	
32816	21	Belmonte, Luigina	7 yrs.	10 Sheafe St. City	Luciano - Lunardina	O		Infantile paralysis	June 7		
32817	21	Conway, Agnes	9 yrs.	11 Williams St, Somerville	John - Margaret	O	7	Infantile Paralysis	May 6	Well	
32818	21	Graziana, Angelina	7 yrs.	351 North St. City	Dead - Carmella	M		Enuresis	Apr.		
32819	21	Gottlieb, Isador	10 yrs.	7 Rochester St. City	Max - Ida	M		Pulmonary T.B.?	May 6	Well	
32820	21	Doherty, Rita	6 yrs.	27 Sidney St. Camb.	Bernard - Mary	M	3	Endocarditis	June 5		
32821	21	Maguire, Francis	5 1/2 yrs.	78 Phillips St, Rox	John - Mary	M		Chorea	July 21		
32822	21	DeRosa, Mary	6 yrs.	57 Lubeck St, E.B.	Arthur - Angie	O		T.B. Ankle	Apr 25		So. Dept
32823	21	[illegible] James		317 Main St [illegible]	[illegible] - Mary			Tonsils [illegible]			

A Register of Patients, 1914. Care expanded to include children with a wide variety of medical and surgical illnesses beyond orthopedic conditions (for example, polio and rheumatic fever) as well as patients recovering from repairs of cleft lips, hernias, and tonsillectomies.

THE WEST END NURSERY, 1881. When Children's Hospital was founded, it did not admit patients under the age of two years. To address this need, the West End Nursery was established in 1881 on Blossom Street, near Massachusetts General Hospital. Dr. Thomas Morgan Rotch was one of two attending physicians on the original staff. Eventually, Rotch became the director of the Infants' Hospital and held that position, as well as physician in chief at Children's Hospital, until his death in 1914.

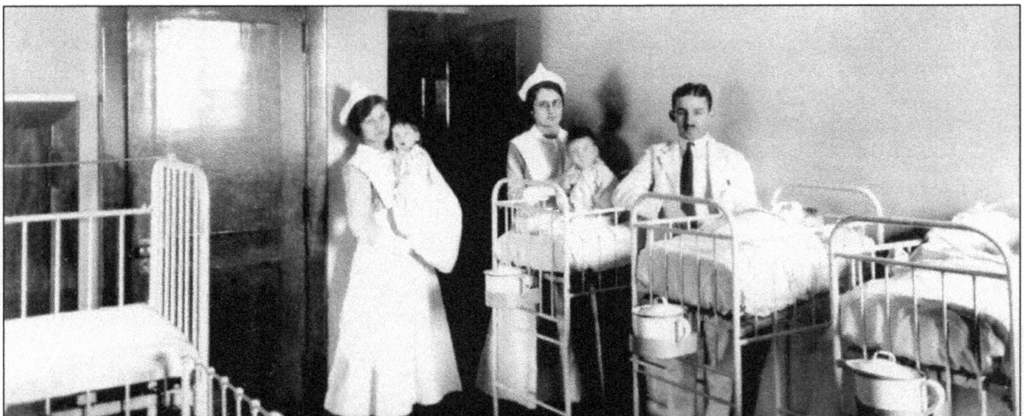

THE INFANTS' HOSPITAL WARD. In 1883, the West End Nursery added "and Infants' Hospital" to its name and described its mission as "the care of disease or alleviation of suffering in children under two years of age." This particular focus made it distinct from Children's Hospital, only two miles away on Huntington Avenue.

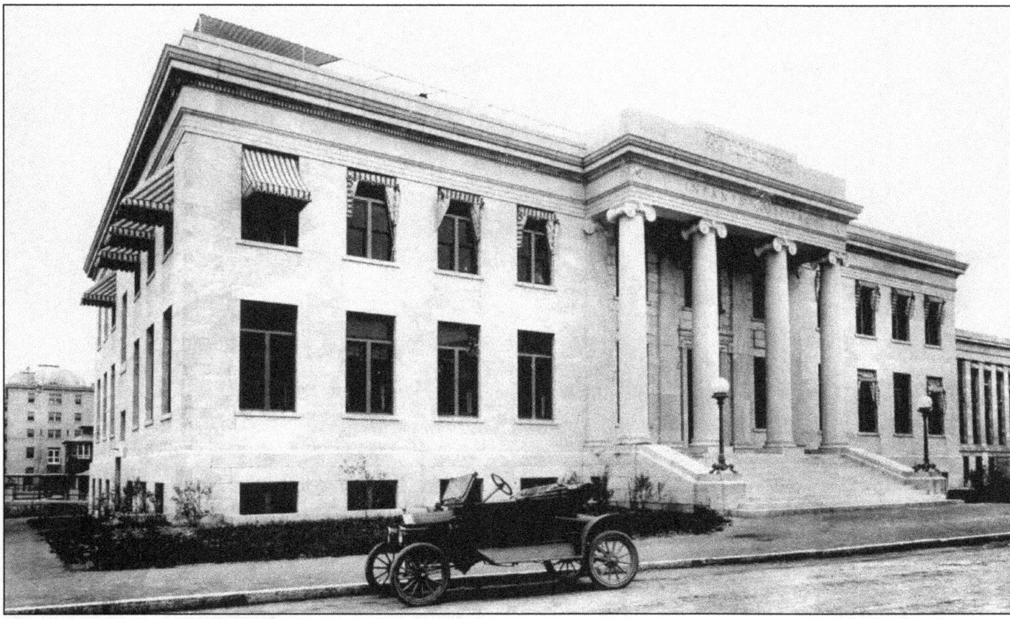

THE NEW INFANTS' HOSPITAL. When Children's Hospital moved to the Longwood area in 1914, the Infants' Hospital relocated to this building on Van Dyke Street (now Shattuck Street). It was named the Thomas Morgan Rotch Jr. Memorial Building in honor of Rotch's deceased son. The building proved ill-suited for efficient hospital use and lacked adequate isolation space. It was sold in 1923 to Harvard University, becoming the Harvard School of Public Health. Later repurchased by Children's Hospital, it now houses administrative offices.

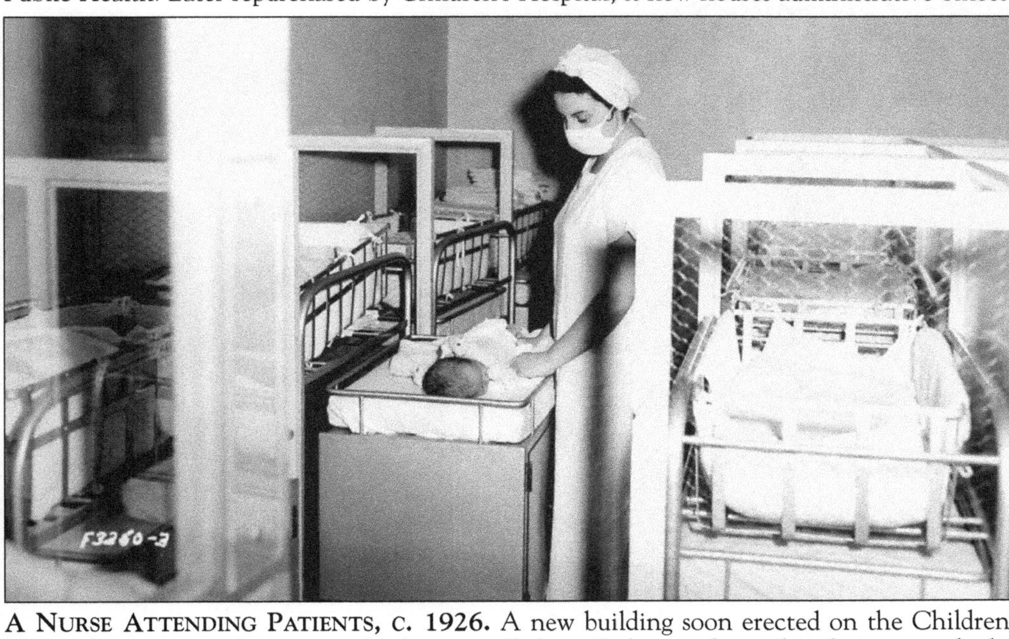

A NURSE ATTENDING PATIENTS, C. 1926. A new building soon erected on the Children's Hospital campus was far superior for the care of babies. Cribs were housed in their own cubicles, and room was provided for a nurse to sit and cradle infants during feedings. The building also included a premature infants' nursery and a sunroom to maximize exposure to natural light.

CHRISTMAS AT THE INFANTS' HOSPITAL, 1931. The Infants' Hospital, like Children's Hospital, made a point of celebrating the holidays in a festive way to spread cheer to its patients, nurses, physicians, and other staff.

A BABY IN A BUCKET. It is bath time at the Infants' Hospital.

CHILDREN'S HOSPITAL, C. 1922. Shortly after the move to Longwood Avenue, Children's Hospital built a number of ward buildings behind the Hunnewell Building. These wards, known as "chicken coops" by those who remember them, were removed for expansion later in the 20th century. One ward, the Ida C. Smith Building, is still in existence. The Infants' Hospital, its original building visible to the far left, relocated to the grounds of the cottage buildings. The two institutions merged officially in 1956. (Courtesy Harvard Medical Library.)

WINTER AT CHILDREN'S HOSPITAL, C. 1920. Small wards were designed to maximize air and light and to minimize the spread of infectious diseases. The central open courtyard contained one small shack for airing mattresses between admissions; this area also served as recreational grounds for patients, nurses, doctors, and other hospital staff.

WARD 1, C. 1930. The patient wards, similarly designed, differed only in size. There were several ward buildings: Medical Ward 1 and Orthopedic Ward 5, two stories each, and Surgical Wards 2 and 4, one story each. There were separate buildings for infants and for surgery. This image shows the two-story Ward 1, with its unheated passage to Ward 2. One of the buildings of Harvard Medical School appears in the background on the right.

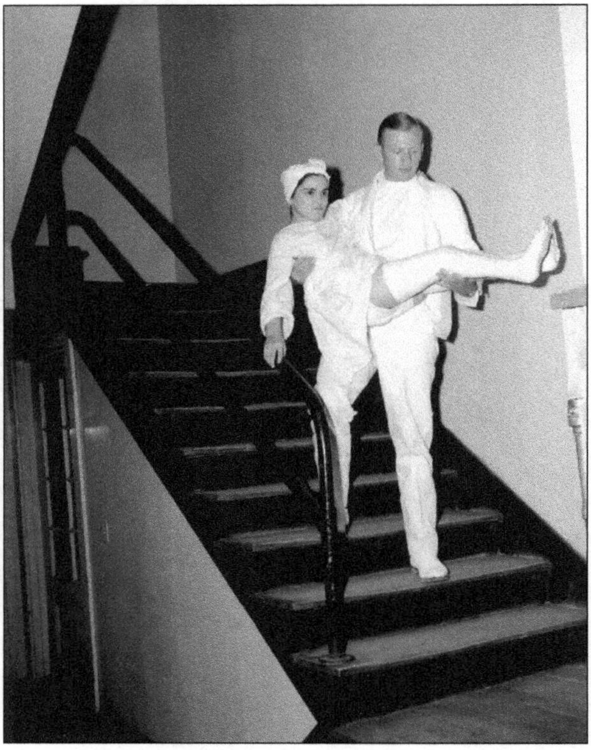

A RESIDENT PHYSICIAN CARRYING A PATIENT. It became clear by the end of the 1920s that Children's Hospital was in great need of modernized facilities. Here, a resident physician carries a young patient with two leg casts down a flight of stairs in the era before elevators were installed.

DR. KENNETH BLACKFAN, 1929. In the long history of Children's Hospital, Dr. Kenneth Blackfan is one of the most renowned figures. Born in Cincinnati, he came to Boston in 1923 from Johns Hopkins Hospital and assumed his duties as the new physician in chief. A quiet, unassuming man, Blackfan was said to be unsurpassed as a bedside teacher. He also had a remarkable eye and memory for clinical details.

MAKING HOSPITAL ROUNDS. Blackfan was appointed the first Thomas Morgan Rotch Professor of Pediatrics at Harvard Medical School. Under his guidance, the physicians' training program at Children's Hospital reached new heights. The old designation of "house pupils" changed to "resident physicians." This cartoon, originally published in the *Journal of Pediatrics*, shows nurses and young physicians doting on Blackfan. Resident physicians came to Children's Hospital following a year or more of an internship and then trained in pediatrics for 15 to 21 months.

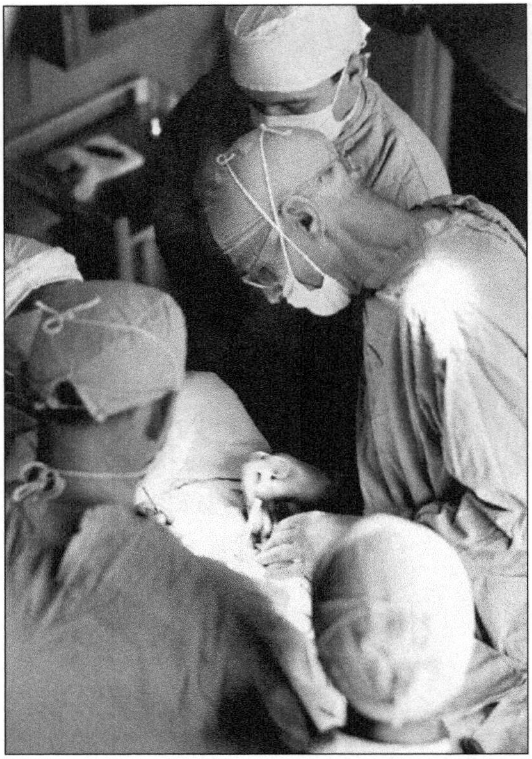

DR. WILLIAM E. LADD. What Blackfan was to medicine, Ladd was to surgery. Pediatric surgery was a new, emerging field, but a few pioneering surgeons at Children's Hospital, led by Ladd (surgeon in chief, 1927–1945), began devoting their careers to it. The William E. Ladd Professor of Child Surgery at Harvard Medical School, established in 1937, was the first of its kind in the nation. Generally considered the founder of modern pediatric surgery, Ladd trained an entire generation of surgeons.

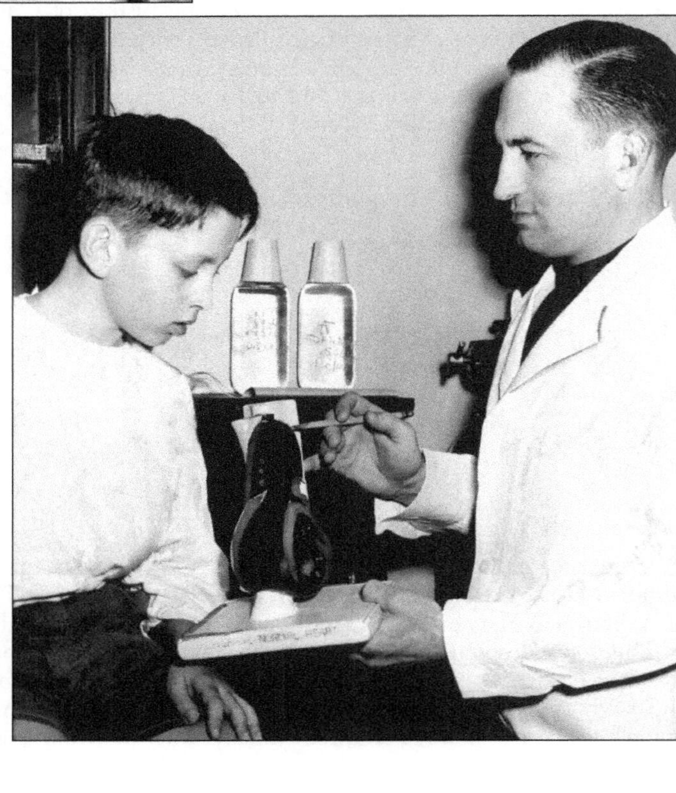

DR. ROBERT E. GROSS. One of Ladd's best-known protégés, Dr. Robert E. Gross also became a seminal figure in the history of pediatric surgery. In 1938, he successfully closed a *patent ductus arteriosus* in a seven-year-old girl who is still alive and well more than 60 years later. This achievement marked the beginning of the new discipline of cardiac surgery. Children's Hospital remains one of the world leaders in this field.

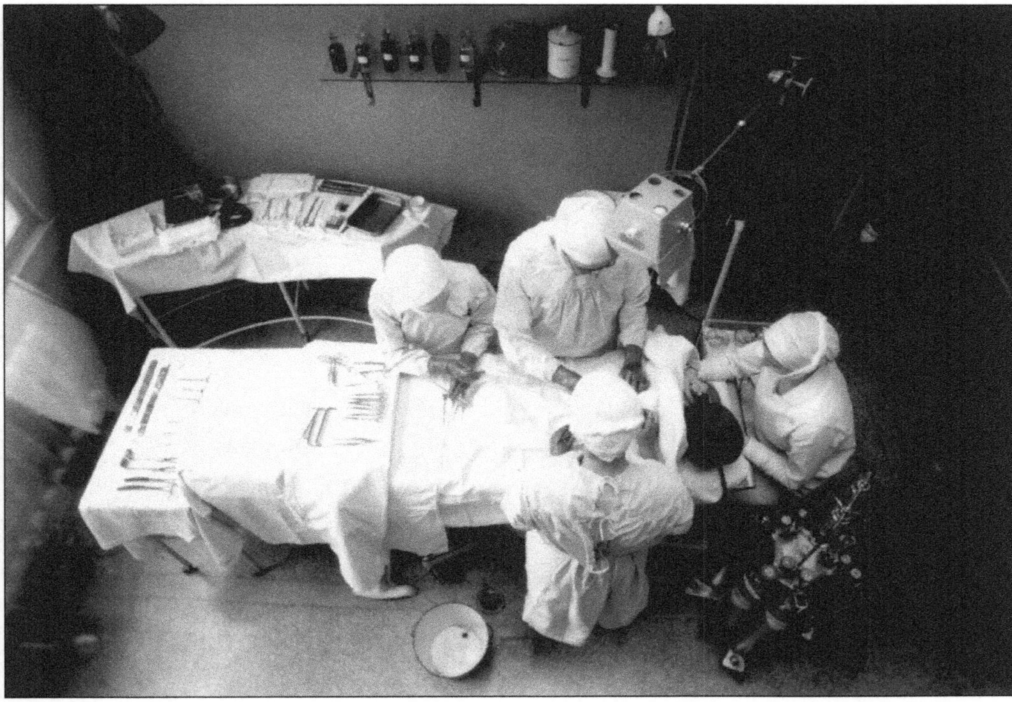

SURGERY. Ladd and his colleagues ushered in many advances in this era. They began to concentrate on surgical conditions in infants and children. Note here that doctors and nurses now wear caps and masks. A primitive anesthesia machine is also visible.

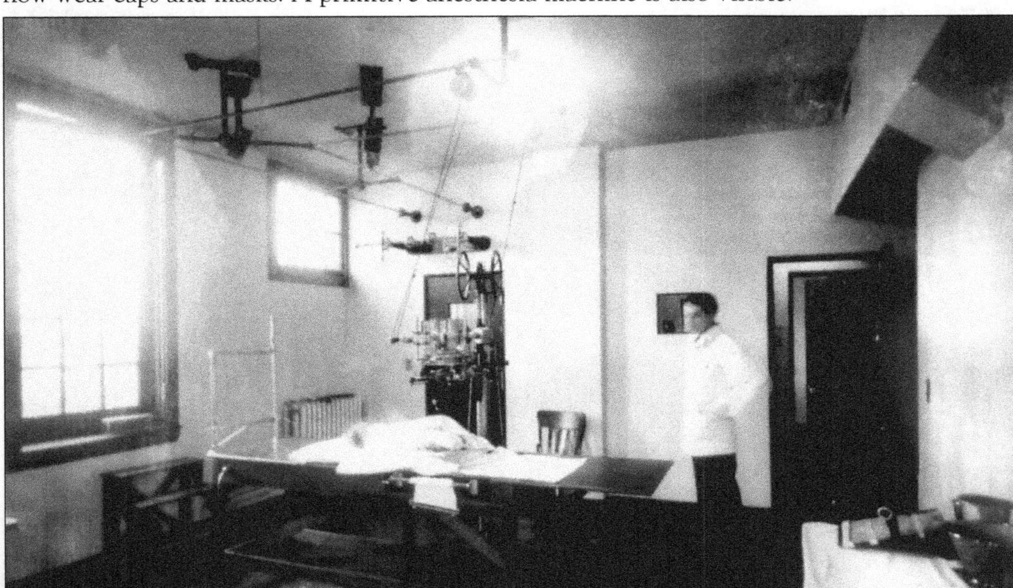

RADIOLOGY. Advances in imaging technology led to radiology becoming an increasingly important aspect of diagnosis. Radiologists worked with surgeons and pediatricians in caring for children with previously untreatable conditions.

Circus Day, 1928. Circus Day was an annual recreational activity at Children's Hospital. Here, the grounds are packed with nurses, patients, doctors, parents, and others affiliated with Children's Hospital. Several people watch from the top of the covered walkway between hospital wards.

Donation Day Activities, 1939. Children's Hospital also held Donation Day functions, which were part of the hospital's fund-raising activities. In 1939, these included charitable events such as a puppet show, seen here, and big-band concerts.

A Hospital Rodeo Event, 1935. In addition to serving as the locale for the circus, the ward grounds became the occasional home to a traveling rodeo. In this photograph, several bed-ridden patients have been brought onto the porch of a ward building to visit with cowgirls and watch trained donkeys perform.

VIPs, 1929. Famous personalities have frequently been visitors to Children's Hospital. Here, Babe Ruth (left) and Will Rogers entertain the children.

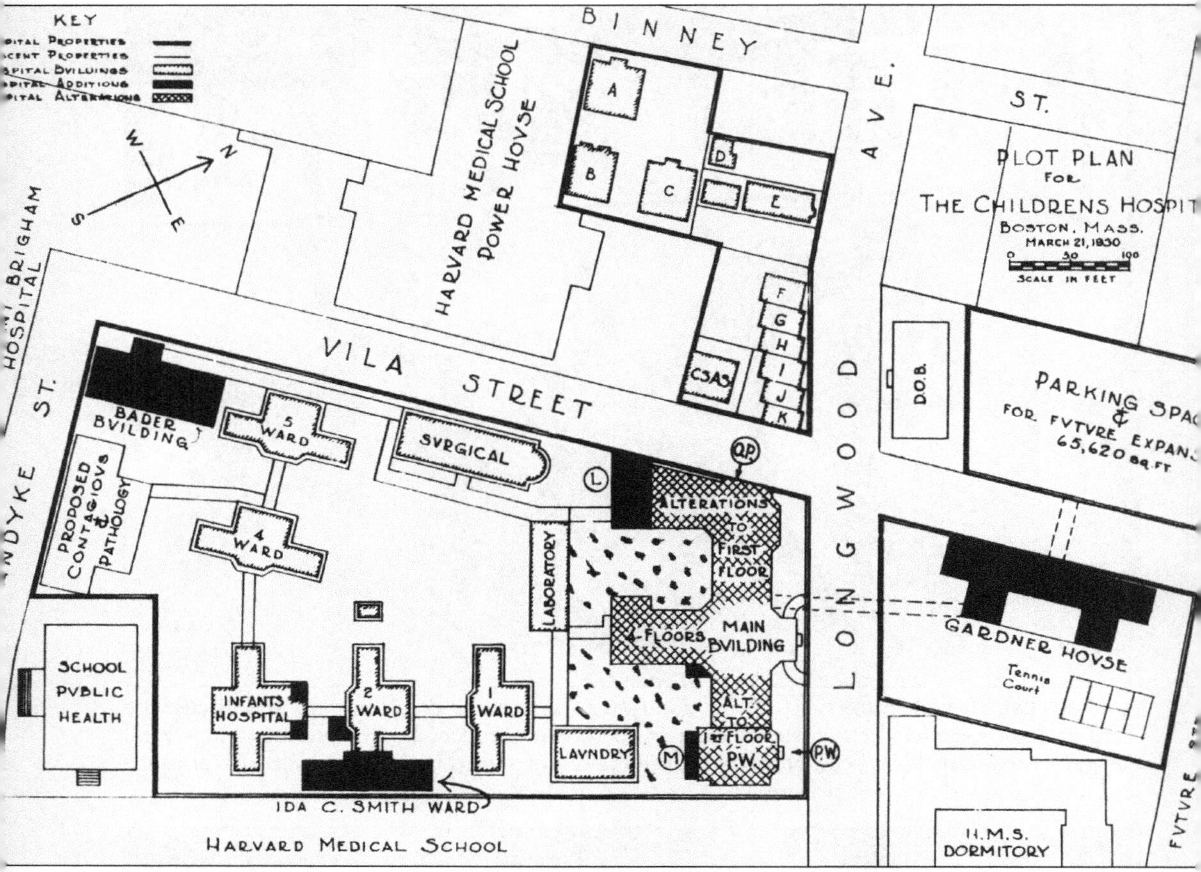

THE EXPANSION PLAN, 1930. Owing to the success of fund-raising activities and to public confidence in the hospital's accomplishments, Children's Hospital began modernizing its physical plant. Three major additions were completed: the Gardner House, which became a new home for nurses and the Children's Hospital School of Nursing; the Bader Building, primarily for patients with neurological problems; and the Ida C. Smith Ward for additional surgical beds. Further expansions included more accommodations for house officers and for "throat patients," of whom greater numbers were admitted than for any other surgical problem.

THE NURSING SCHOOL GROUNDBREAKING, 1929. Construction of a new building for the School of Nursing was one of the most significant additions to the hospital. In this photograph, George Peabody Gardner (far left), after whom the building was named, oversees the groundbreaking ceremony. Superintendent Ida C. Smith, RN (left), and director of nursing Stella Goostray, RN (right), stand adjacent to Olga (Mrs. George) Monks, another member of the Gardner family.

THE GARDNER HOUSE, 1931. By 1921, it had become necessary to convert the nurses' wing of the Hunnewell Building into a private ward. A new nurses' residence, the Gardner House, opened on May 26, 1930, on Longwood Avenue opposite the Hunnewell Building. "At six-thirty that morning, an army of young women, each with a blanket under her arm, left the Hotel Harvard—a red-letter day in the history of the Children's Hospital School of Nursing."

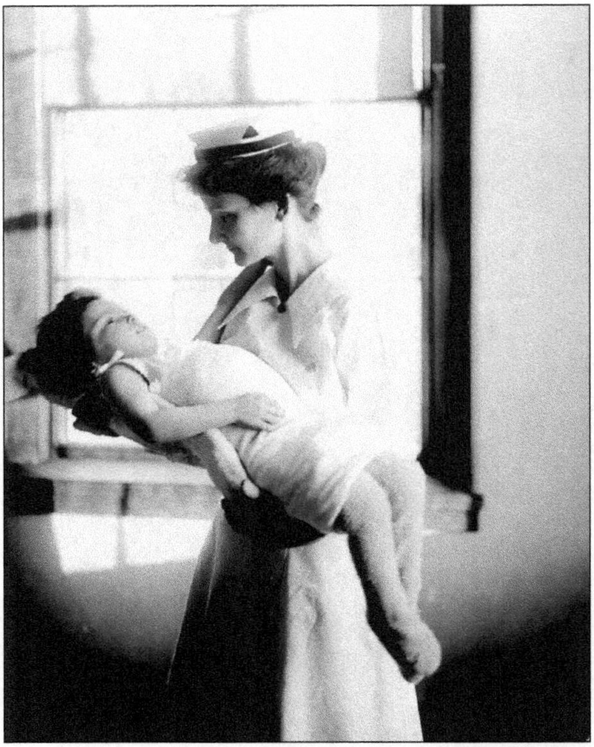

A Nursing School Graduate, c. 1930. Graduates of the Children's Hospital School of Nursing went on to serve in many hospitals throughout the Boston area and greater New England. Their care and dedication is evident in this image from the Wellesley Convalescent Home.

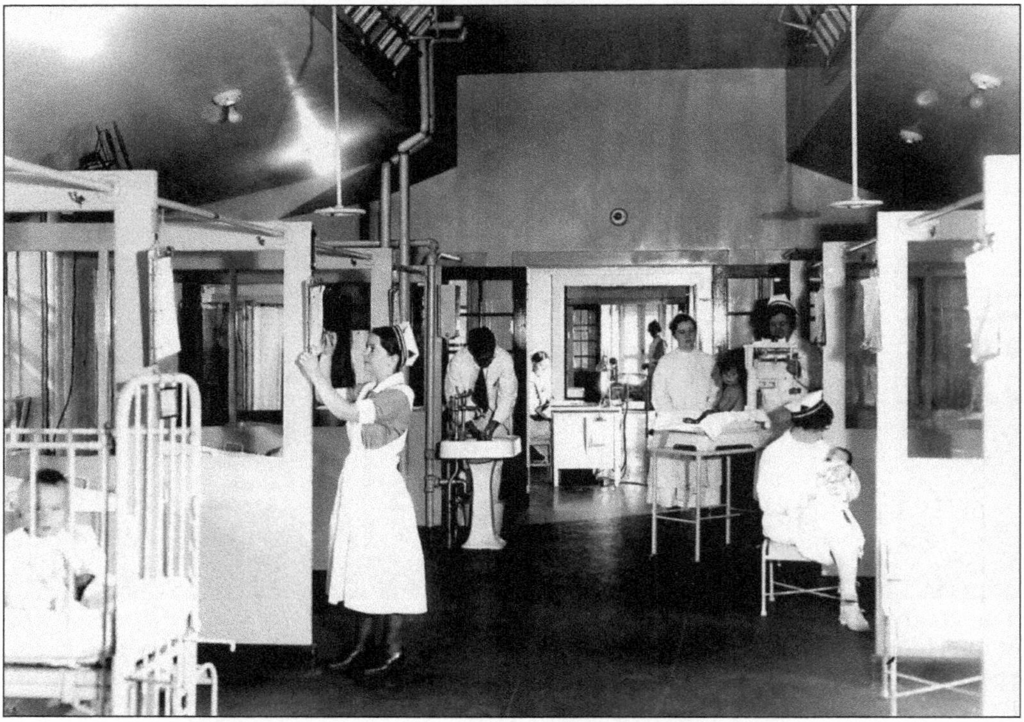

Care on the Wards. Nursing school students care for patients in the Infants' Hospital cubicles.

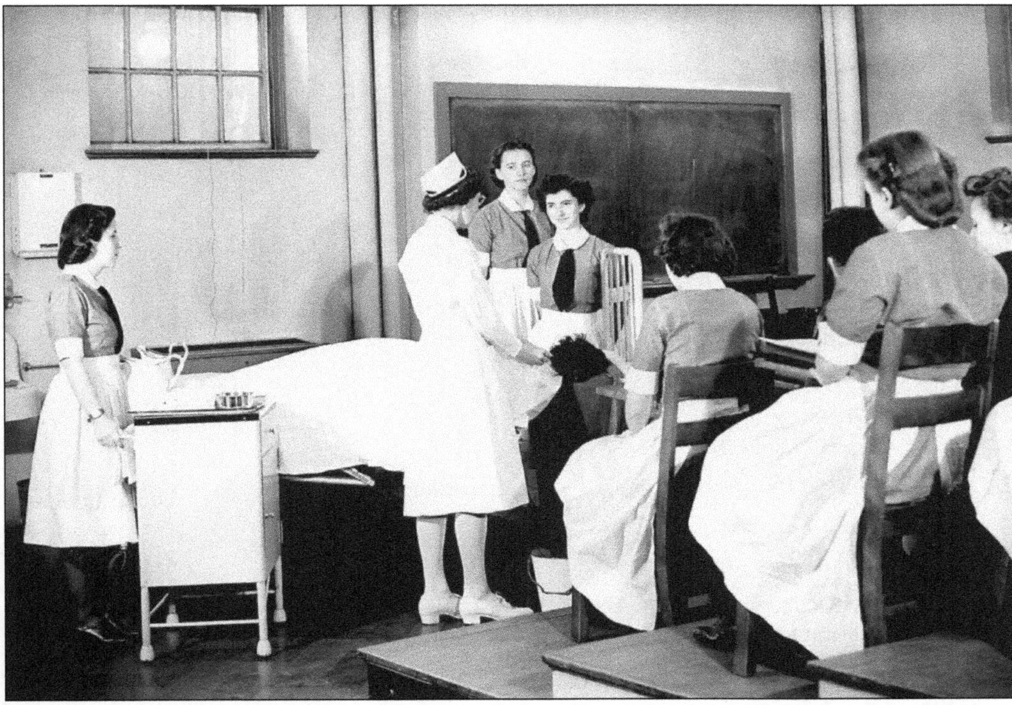

GARDNER HOUSE CLASSROOMS. The new home of the School of Nursing provided living accommodations for 225 nurses, a nine-room infirmary, numerous sitting rooms, recreation rooms, a chapel, a library, a grand living room, and, of course, classrooms.

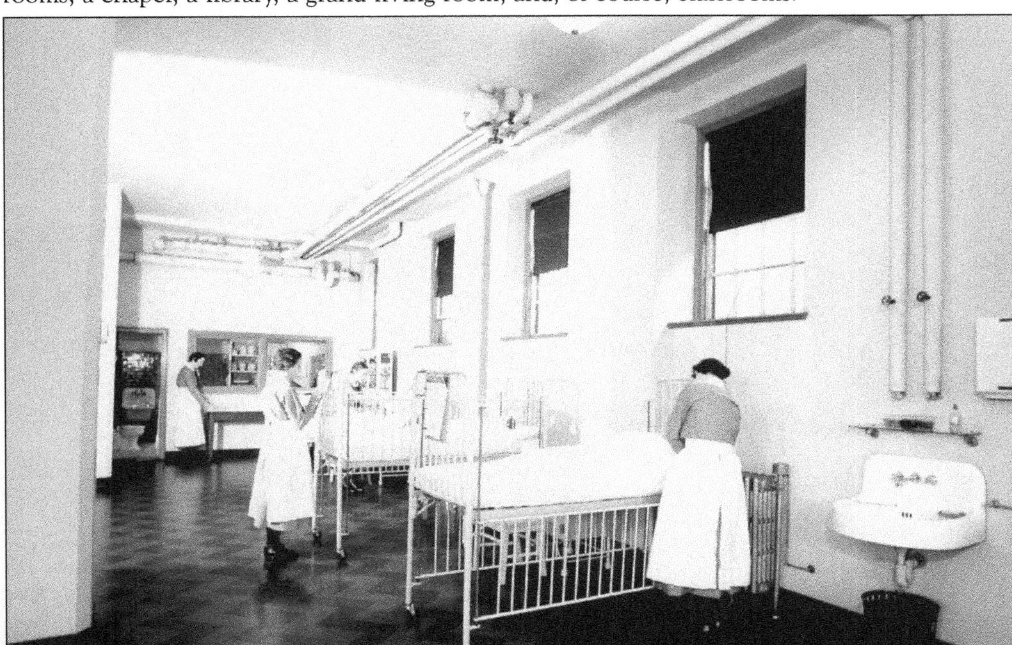

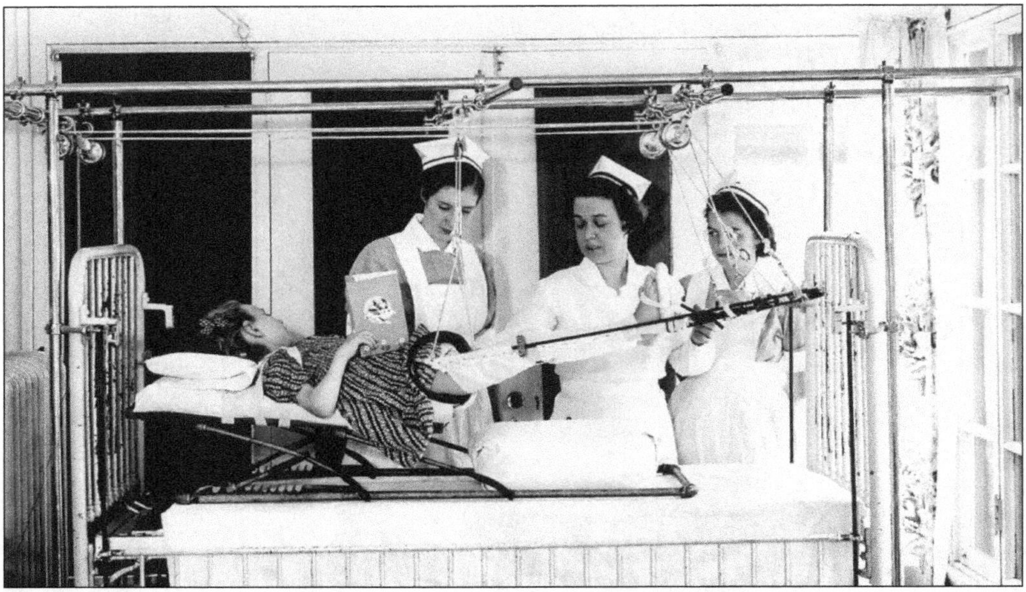

NURSING INSTRUCTION AT THE BEDSIDE. Classroom teaching was supplemented with instruction in caring for patients on the wards, the hallmark of physician and nursing education at Children's Hospital.

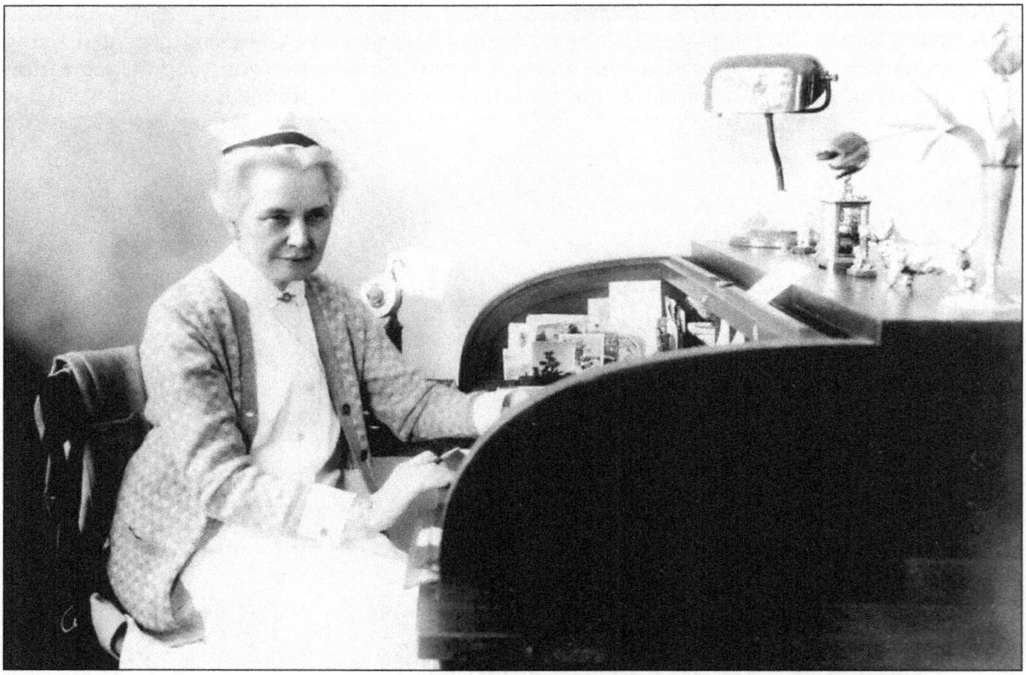

IDA C. SMITH, RN, 1917. A graduate of the Children's Hospital School of Nursing class of 1891 and hospital superintendent from 1917 to 1932, Ida C. Smith was one of the most respected figures in this early period. She was the last of the "lady superintendents" and "ruled benignantly and effectively." Her name continues to be memorialized at Children's Hospital in the Ida C. Smith Building.

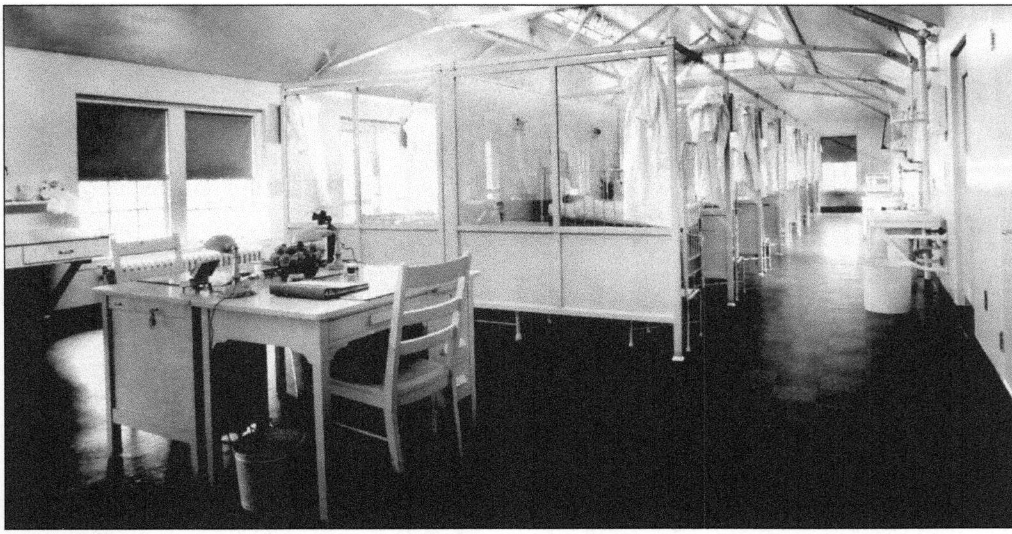

The Interior of the Ida C. Smith Building, 1930s. This ward, erected in 1930, was committed to the surgical care of infants and contained 28 bassinets and cribs. The majority of patients originally treated in this ward were brought over from the Infants' Hospital, located at the rear of the building, further evidence of the close relationship between the two hospitals. As the only remaining pavilion on the Children's Hospital campus today, the Ida C. Smith Building now functions, in part, as a poison-control center, begun in 1955.

Stella Goostray, RN. A dedicated and energetic graduate of the Children's Hospital Nursing School in 1919, Goostray served as superintendent of nurses and director of the School of Nursing from 1927 to 1946. A nationally known leader, she was instrumental in creating higher standards for nursing education throughout the United States.

THE BADER AND CARNEGIE BUILDINGS, 1930. The opening of the Bader Building in May 1930 ushered in a remarkable era of clinical research. Built adjacent to Orthopedic Ward 5, the new six-story structure was used primarily as a special unit for children with neuromuscular diseases and as an expansion for the old Laboratory Study Building. Behind the Bader, the three-story Carnegie Building (left) is visible. Purchased by Children's Hospital in 1945, it housed additional medical and surgical research laboratories and was where Dr. John Enders, Dr. Frederick Robbins, and Dr. Thomas Weller did their seminal work on poliovirus. It was demolished in 2001.

THE BADER POOL. The first two floors of the Bader Building housed the Physical Therapy Department, as well as a gymnasium and hydrotherapy pool for polio patients. Before the 1930 opening of the Bader pool, polio patients received treatment in a therapeutic tank. In both cases, water support made muscle movements easier.

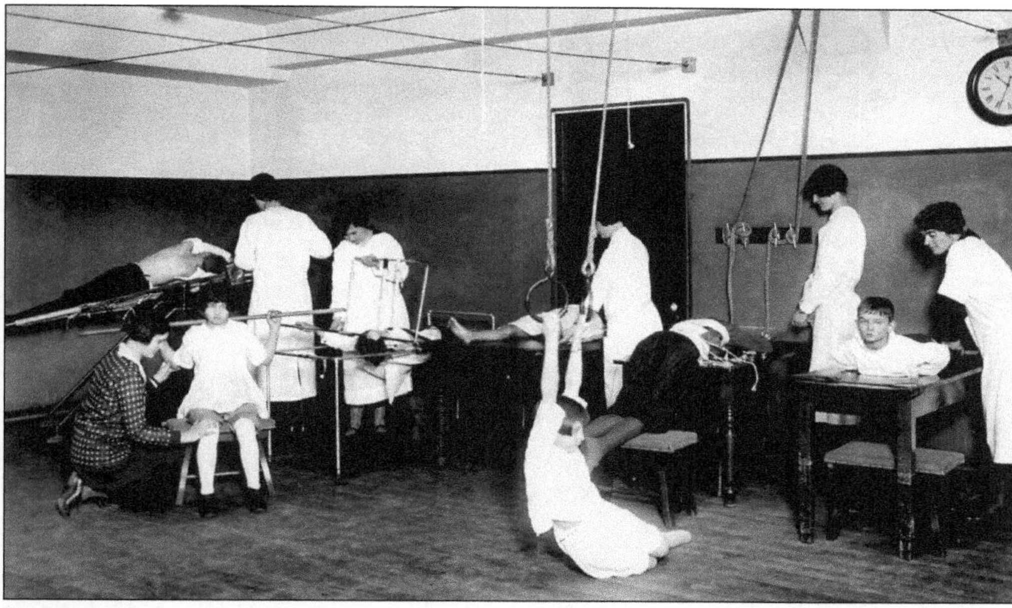

THE GYMNASIUM, C. 1925. Beginning in 1882, the Orthopedic Department used a gymnasium to help treat disabled patients. It was equipped with many devices to aid in rehabilitation. This photograph shows the gymnastic room in Orthopedic Ward 5 and a number of patients "slowly but surely getting straightened out," according to a fund-raising brochure of the time.

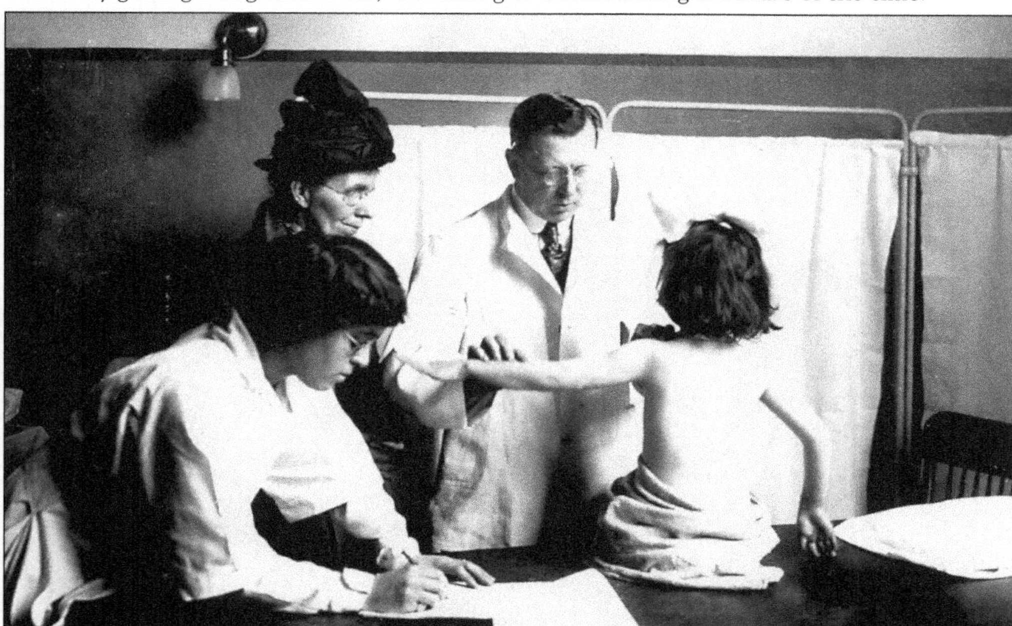

DR. ARTHUR T. LEGG, C. 1930. Children with orthopedic conditions were common in the hospital, and Dr. Arthur T. Legg followed in the footsteps of Dr. Edward Bradford in pioneering their treatment. Legg's career as the director of the orthopedic clinic helped promote new treatments for orthopedic diseases, and he is remembered for his efforts in treating children with polio.

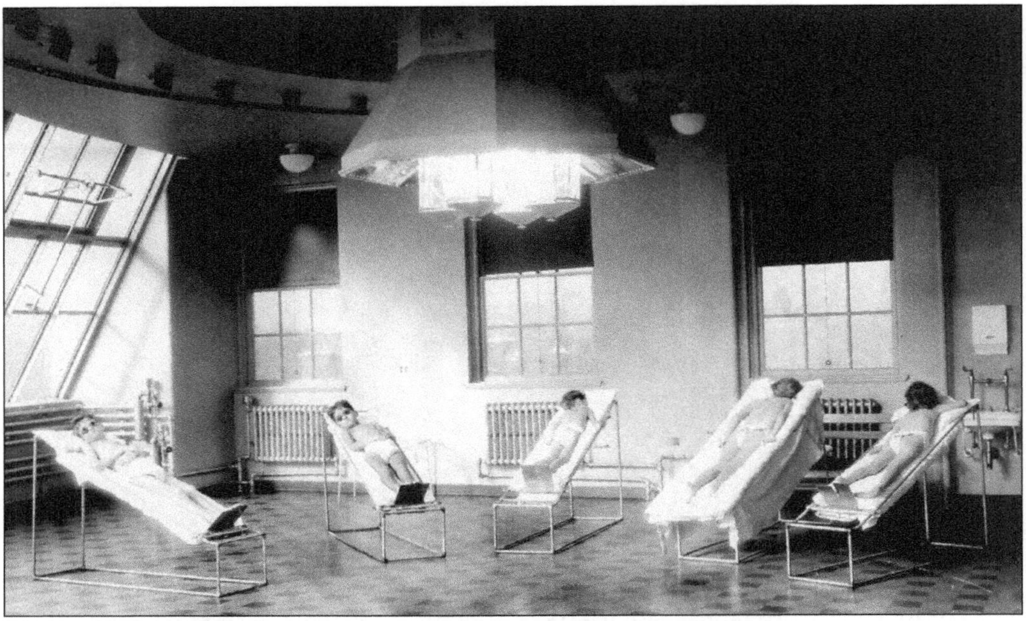

THE BADER SOLARIUM, 1930S. Sunlight was considered very important in the treatment of many diseases, especially rickets (a disease resulting from a lack of vitamin D or calcium). Here, several children receive carbon arc and ultraviolet light treatments. The risk of prolonged ultraviolet light exposure as a cause of skin cancer was not appreciated in that era.

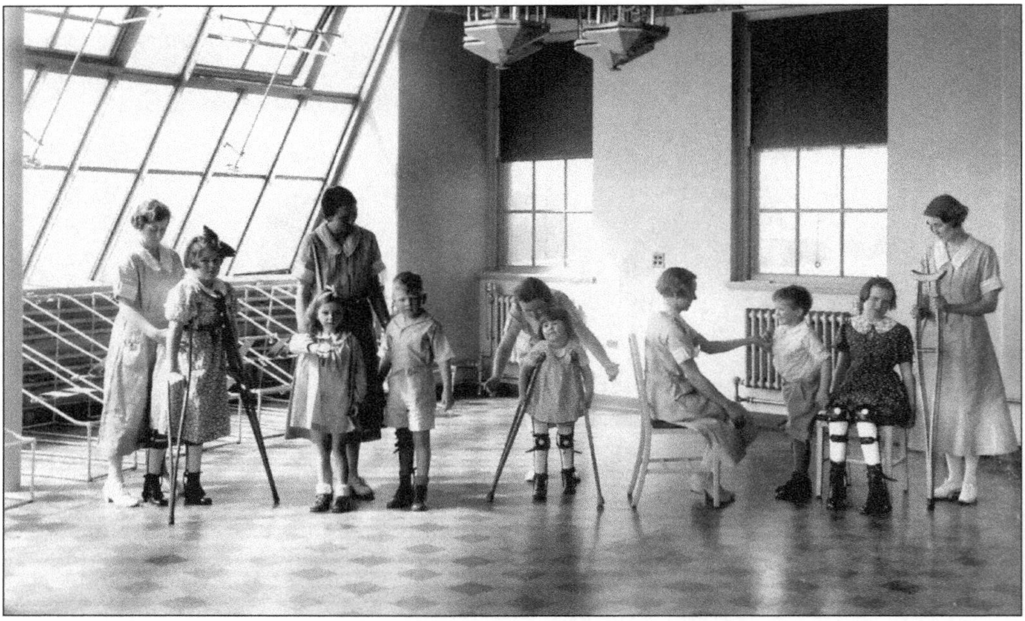

PHYSICAL THERAPY. Physical therapy has a long history at Children's Hospital as a way to restore function. Before moving to Longwood Avenue, the hospital performed most physical therapy to restore strength and movement because of bone and joint tuberculosis. With pasteurization of milk, however, tuberculosis was largely eliminated in the United States, replaced by infantile paralysis (polio) as the primary disabling disease.

OCCUPATIONAL THERAPY, 1939. Occupational therapy involved different activities, including games, crafts, and schooling for patients who were hospitalized for prolonged periods of time.

THE LIBRARY, C. 1935. The portable library was one of the favorite activities of both patients and families and was supplied with generous donations of books. The "librarians" were Children's Hospital volunteers. Today, well-stocked libraries exist for medical professionals and families alike.

DR. PHILIP DRINKER, INVENTOR OF THE IRON LUNG. Infantile paralysis—or poliomyelitis, better known as polio—was one of the most feared scourges in the first half of the 20th century. In the Boston area, the Harvard Infantile Paralysis Commission turned to Children's Hospital both for help in caring for children who had contracted polio and in an effort to find a cure. It was within this context that Philip Drinker of the Harvard School of Public Health developed the iron lung in 1928.

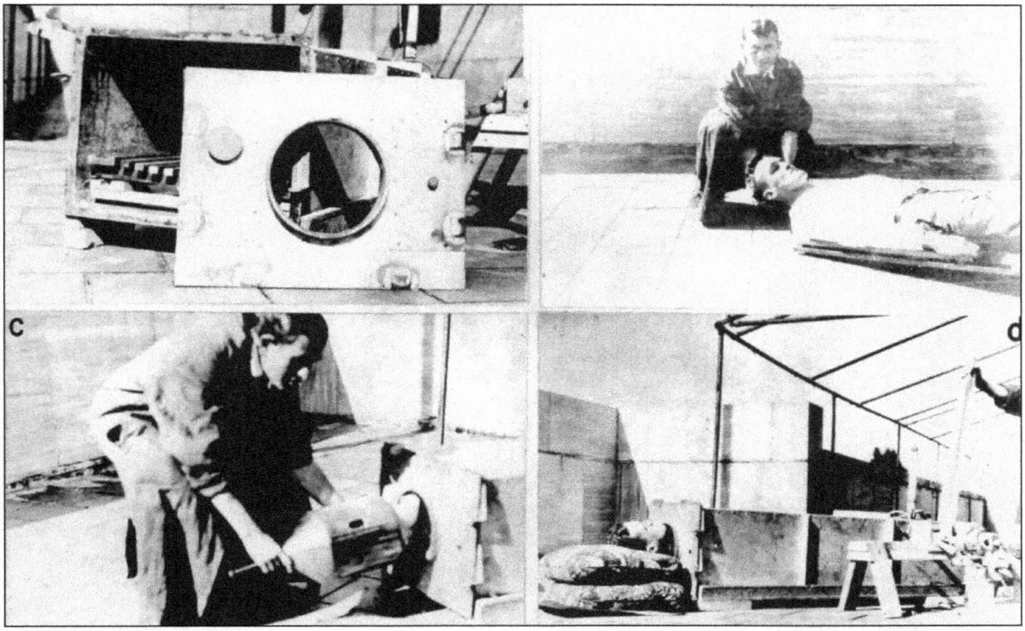

AN EARLY IRON LUNG, LATE 1920S. Dr. Philip Drinker's associate Dr. James Wilson demonstrates the use of the iron lung. By 1932, both the Children's and Infants' Hospitals were using the new technology to assist patients with their breathing.

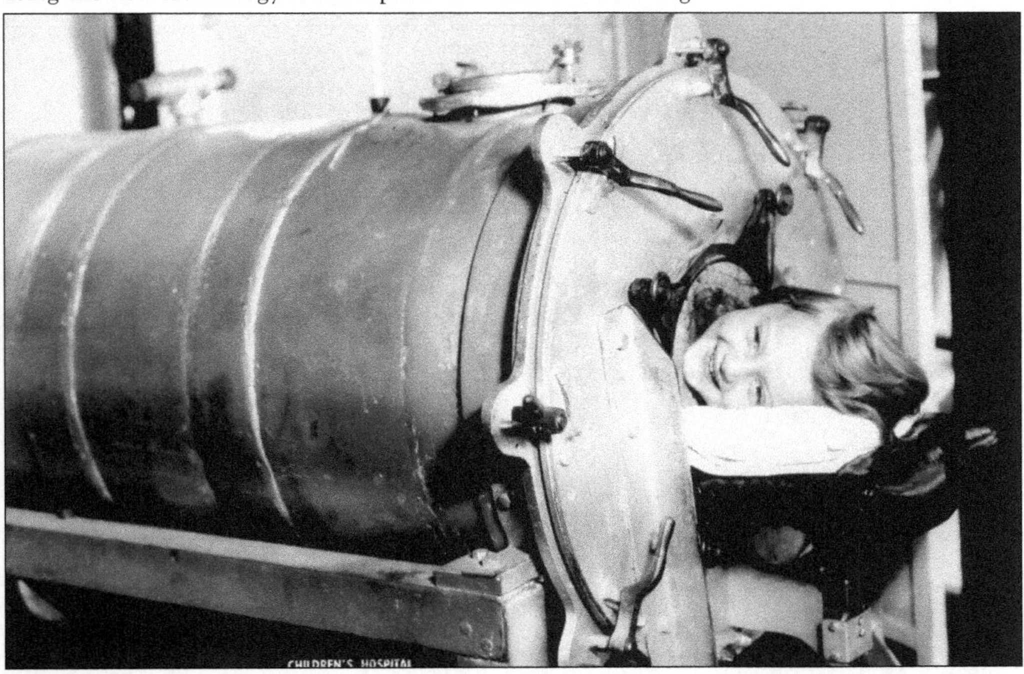

A SINGLE-CHILD IRON LUNG RESPIRATOR, EARLY 1930S. The new respirators were in great demand in Boston and throughout the United States. Polio epidemics, however, continued to bring patients to both the Children's and Infants' Hospitals. The huge demand for respirators threatened to outstrip the number of iron lung machines available.

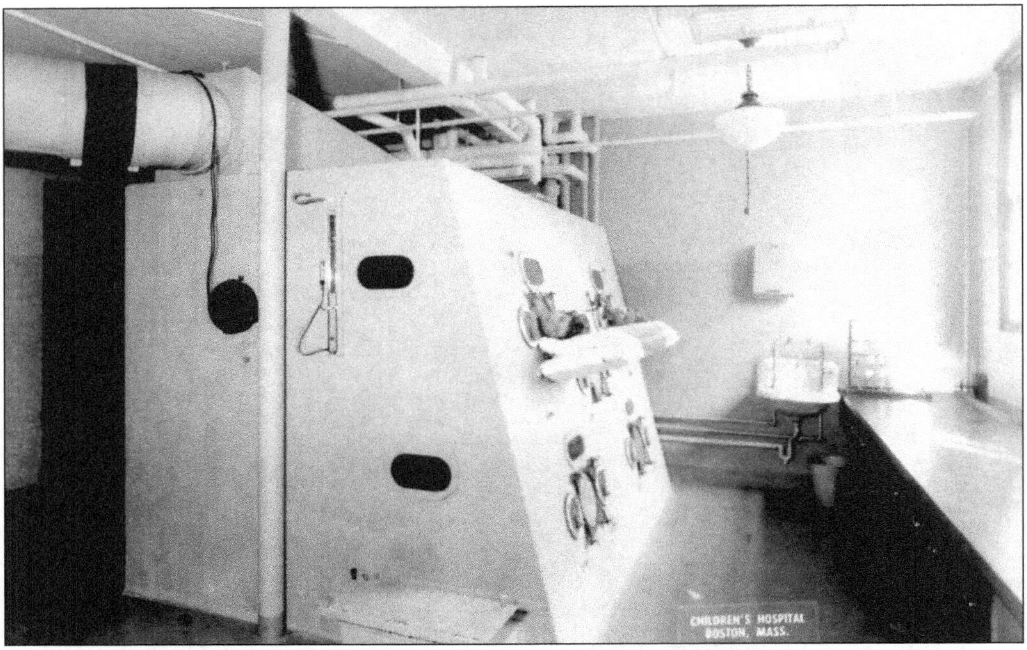

A Room-Sized Respirator, 1933. To help meet the demand, Children's Hospital built a room-sized respirator in the basement of the old Infants' Hospital building in 1932. In 1933, there were 49 admissions for polio, and in 1935, 146 admissions.

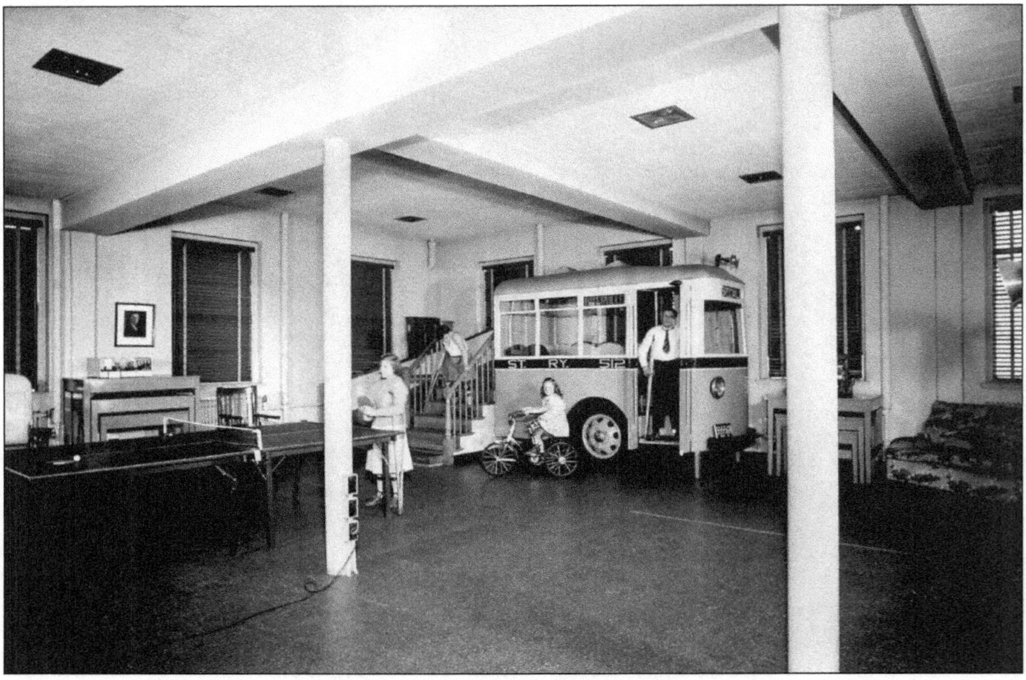

The Bader Functional Room, Early 1940s. The sixth floor of the Bader Building contained three major areas for physiotherapy. In this room, patients learned to manage daily activities in a capable manner.

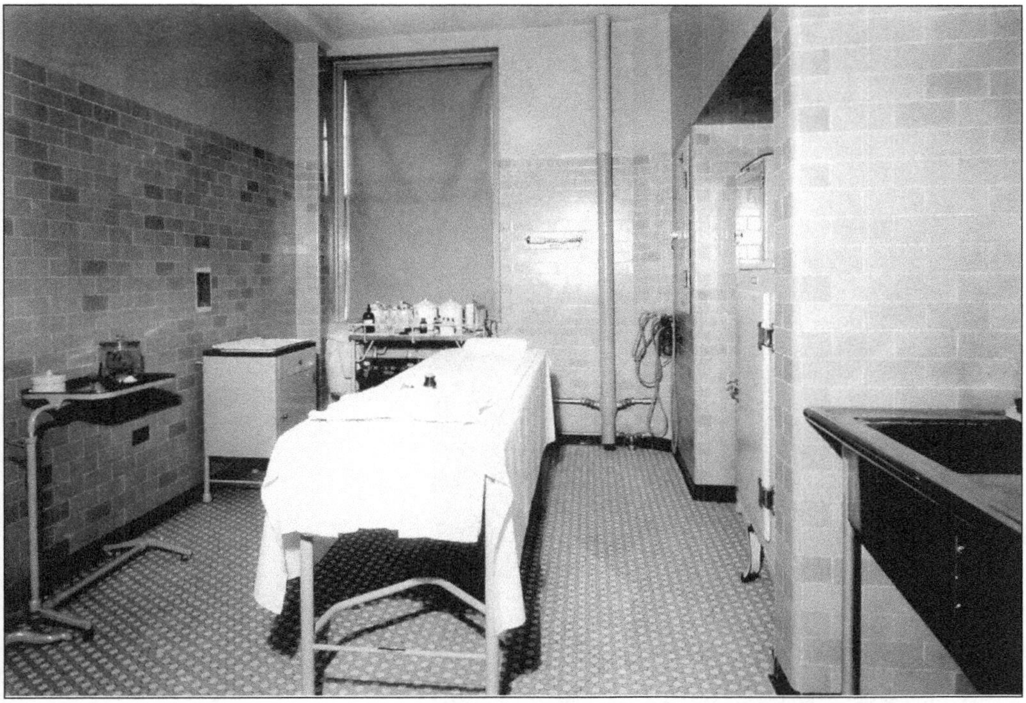

Early Treatment Rooms, c. 1930. Patients with infectious diseases were housed in the isolation unit adjacent to the Bader Building, to which the unit was later connected.

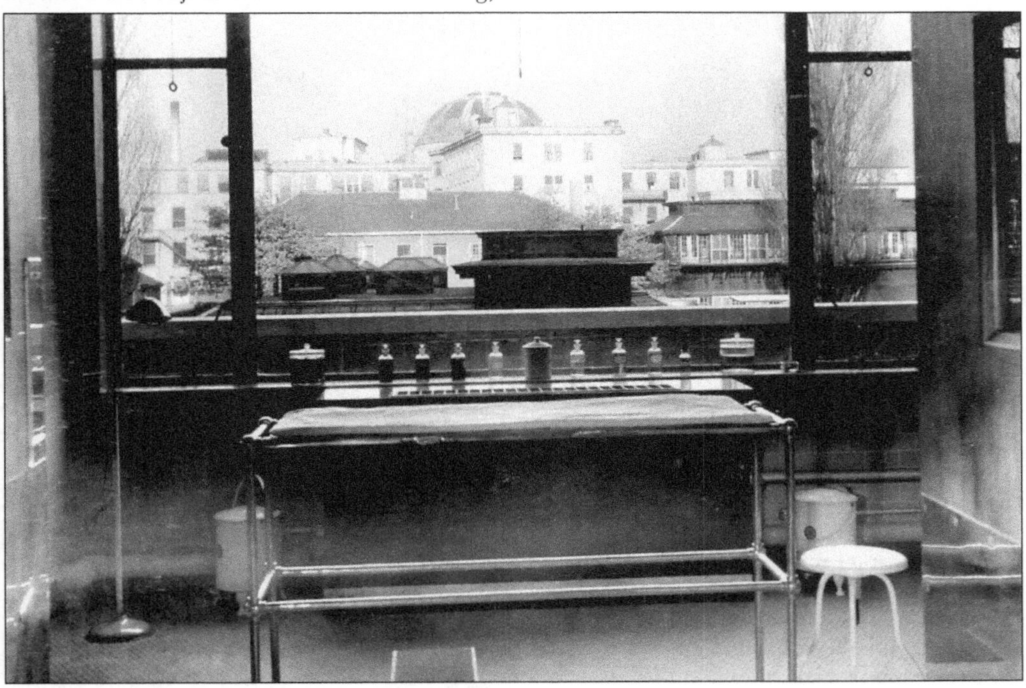

Dr. S. Burt Wolbach. The isolation ward and laboratories, established in 1915 at a cost of $200, developed from the modest laboratory of Wolbach, who was appointed pathologist in chief that same year. The new ward and other improvements served as the springboard for pathological research. This included the work of Wolbach's successor, Dr. Sidney Farber, who developed the first successful chemotherapy for children's cancer.

Dr. James L. Gamble. Dr. James L. Gamble worked at Children's Hospital from 1921 to the early 1950s. He was the first Children's Hospital pediatrician to devote his career to pediatric research and, specifically, to an understanding of the body's fluids and electrolytes. His remarkable book *Clinical Anatomy, Physiology, and Pathology of Extra-Cellular Fluid* led to effective intravenous fluid treatment for childhood diarrhea.

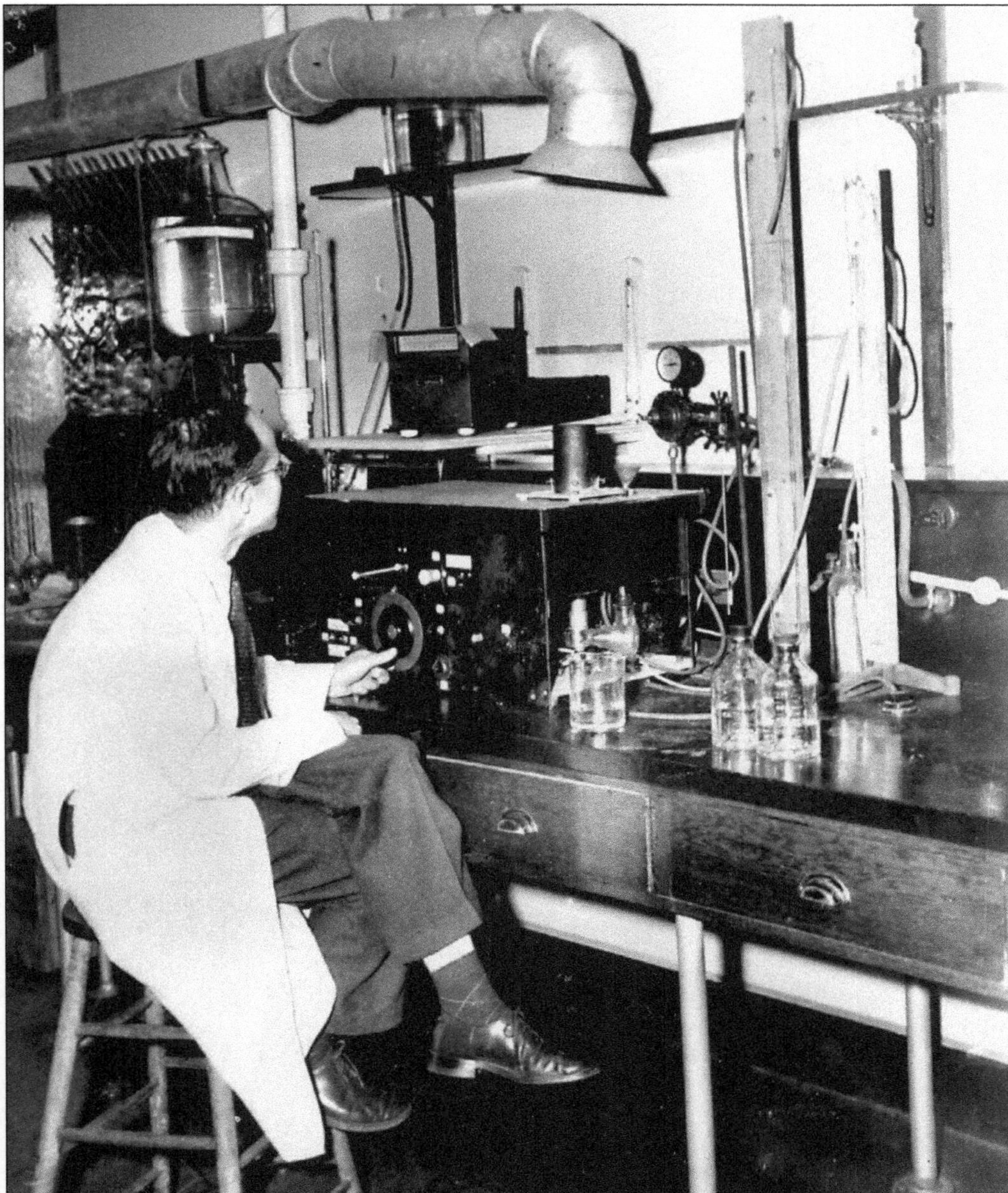

THE LABORATORY STUDY BUILDING, C. 1930. Located behind the Hunnewell Building in the hospital yard, the Laboratory Study Building was constructed in 1921, with additions in 1926. This research facility became the personal laboratory of Gamble and also served as a library for the clinical and research staff. It provided working space, as seen here, for some of the most distinguished researchers in chemistry, hematology, nutrition, and bacteriology until it was razed in 1964. Gamble's library has been largely reassembled as the Gamble Reading Room, currently located in the hospital library.

THE CLINICAL BACTERIOLOGY LABORATORY, 1937. In the 1930s, Children's Hospital assumed a leading role in clinical research and the use of antibiotics in the treatment of children. Many infections of the time proved fatal until 1937, when a six-year-old girl was successfully treated with a new sulfa drug imported from Germany. A few years later, Children's Hospital physicians began using the newly developed antibiotic: penicillin.

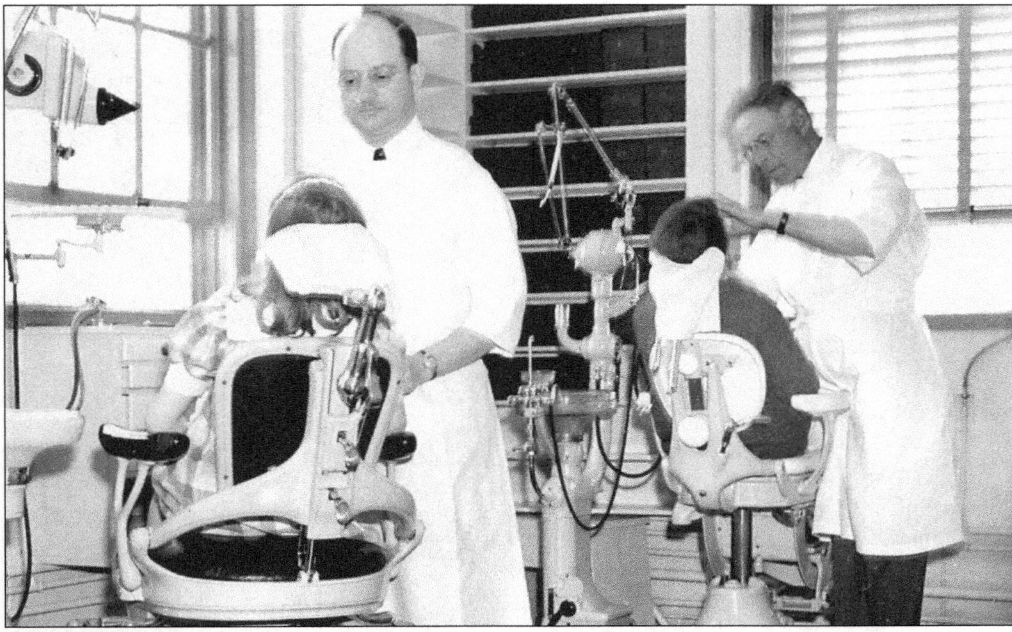

THE DENTAL CLINIC. Dentists have been vital in Children's Hospital's efforts to treat pediatric patients. In addition to providing routine dental care, dentists treated children with major craniofacial problems. In 1935, Paul Losch, DMD, arrived at Children's Hospital, where he remained until 1969. His work led to the development of the Department of Pediatric Dentistry.

DR. BRONSON CROTHERS AND PEDIATRIC NEUROLOGY. The fourth and fifth floors of the Bader Building, known as Ward 9, were dedicated to the work of Dr. Bronson Crothers, who investigated many problems, from birthing injuries to congenital nervous system anomalies. In addition to his pioneering work in cerebral palsy, Crothers and his successors developed revolutionary approaches to treating behavioral disorders, emphasizing "concern for the personality of the patient."

DR. HARVEY CUSHING AND NEUROSURGERY. Dr. Harvey Cushing treated Children's Hospital patients who needed neurosurgical procedures at the adjacent Peter Bent Brigham Hospital, where he was appointed first surgeon in chief in 1913. Generally considered the father of modern neurosurgery, Cushing was a true renaissance man. As well as being a gifted artist, he won a Pulitzer Prize in 1926 for his biography of the famous physician Sir William Osler. (Courtesy Harvard Medical Library.)

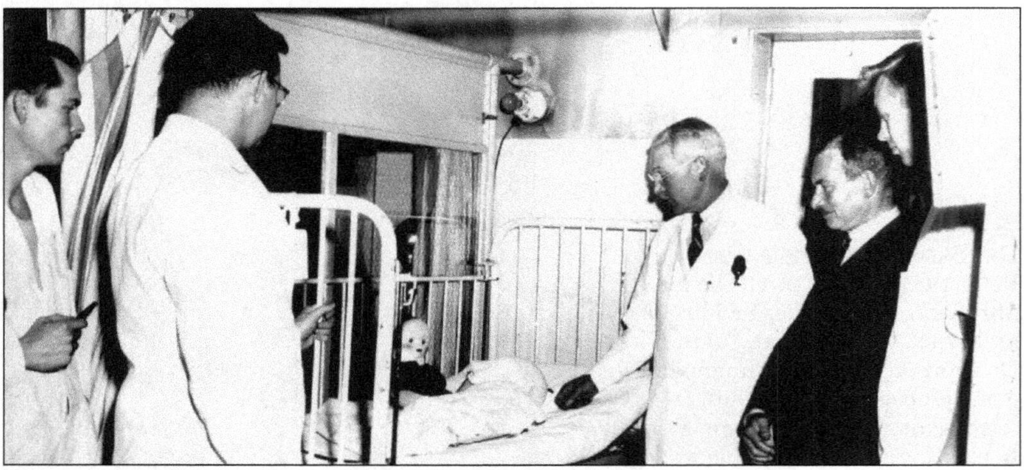

DR. FRANC INGRAHAM AND PEDIATRIC NEUROSURGERY. After training with Cushing, Dr. Franc Ingraham (center) became a neurosurgeon at Children's Hospital in 1929. He served jointly at Children's and Peter Bent Brigham Hospital, located across Shattuck Street. Meticulous and comprehensive, Ingraham's work focused on the treatment of several neurosurgical conditions affecting newborns and young children.

A DAY'S WORK IS NEVER DONE, C. 1940. Children's Hospital has never simply consisted of the efforts of doctors and nurses. It would not have succeeded without the devoted support and great effort of legions of men and women. They work behind the scenes doing the unspectacular, often unrecognized work, of maintenance, washing, ironing, communications, groundskeeping, and innumerable other essential functions.

OUTPATIENT PARKING. Today, parking cars in the Longwood Medical area can be a challenge. In the 1930s, it was carriages that clogged the sidewalk, as seen here adjacent to the Hunnewell Building. The Gardner House is visible in the background.

THE OUTPATIENT CLINIC, 1930S. Children's Hospital managers organized the Department of Outpatients in 1874 and rented a small house for the clinic in 1875. The value and success of this department was continually reflected in the increasing census of patients. This 1930s photograph shows a long line of patients and parents and wooden benches, a scene very familiar to many families.

Four

FRIENDS AND ASSOCIATIONS

1869–1946

Today, it is common for many hospitals to arrange themselves in "networks," sets of relationships with other healthcare institutions that, taken as a whole, help provide a "continuum of care."

The concept is not new to Children's Hospital, which has long benefitted from the friendship and partnership of many other institutions, associations that were based first on charitable and then on clinical principles. The hospital's relationship with Harvard Medical School has already been noted, but there were many others as well.

The Sisters of St. Margaret began their long connection with Children's Hospital in 1872 and provided care for patients as well as training for new nurses. Another group, the Ladies' Aid Association, was organized around the time of the hospital's founding and for many years purchased food, supplies, and toys for the young patients. The Ladies' Aid Association also supported Children's Hospital's convalescent home, located first in Weston and then in Wellesley, where children had the opportunity to recover in an environment less intense than an inpatient hospital. This was especially important because at that time patients were commonly hospitalized for months.

Children's Hospital also enjoyed a close relationship with the West End Nursery (later the Infants' Hospital), opening in 1881. At that time, Children's Hospital, like most pediatric facilities, did not admit patients under two years of age; therefore, the West End Nursery played an important role in attempting to provide care for infants and toddlers in Boston. With Dr. Thomas Morgan Rotch being appointed physician in chief at both institutions, and with the simultaneous relocation of the Infants' and Children's Hospitals to Longwood Avenue in 1914, the two became clinically integrated (see chapter 3).

Children's Hospital also forged strong bonds with many other institutions serving children in the Boston area. Among others, these included the House of the Good Samaritan, the Sharon Sanatorium, the Sarah Fuller School for Little Deaf Children, the Judge Baker Children's Center, and many of the other Harvard-affiliated hospitals. Today, Children's Hospital Boston, although still freestanding and independent, has countless community, regional, national, and international partners in patient care, education, and research.

The Children's Mission. This box was used to collect money to provide housing and care for Massachusetts orphans. Early hospital records show that a number of patients at Children's Hospital, particularly in the early years, came from the Children's Mission. It is now known as the Parents' and Children's Services at Children's Hospital Boston.

The Ladies' Aid Association. Part of Children's Hospital from its inception, the Ladies' Aid Association provided "linen, towels, children's clothes . . . as well as pictures, toys, books, . . . and [money] to aid us in paying some of our bills." Occasionally, these donations included small pets, such as the rabbit shown here. The Ladies' Aid Association was established at the suggestion of the hospital managers but operated independently. Today, its work is carried on by the Children's Hospital League.

THE CONVALESCENT HOME. In 1874, the managers rented a house in Weston, where children could receive "the benefit of country air." Three years later, the Ladies' Aid Association assumed responsibility for the building, and by 1882, it had become an extension of Children's Hospital itself. The Convalescent Home grew rapidly; in 1890, it expanded to 33 acres of land on Forest Street in Wellesley. It remained open all year after 1894 and primarily served as a fresh-air treatment facility for children with tuberculosis.

THE CONVALESCENT HOME BUILDINGS. Destroyed by fire in 1903, the Forest Street home was rebuilt with a capacity of 100 patients. By the end of the 1930s, with the increasing use of private transportation, as well as the availability of antibiotics, patients were no longer housed for prolonged periods of time. In addition, the home was too far from Boston for satisfactory medical supervision. In 1958, the Convalescent Home closed.

OPEN-AIR TREATMENT, C. 1927. The Convalescent Home featured 20- by 40-foot wooden buildings and sliding doors kept open even during the winter to let in as much fresh air as possible for "nervous patients." In addition, children were regularly wheeled outdoors in go-carts to benefit from sunlight. These buildings were heated by constantly stoked coal-burning stoves.

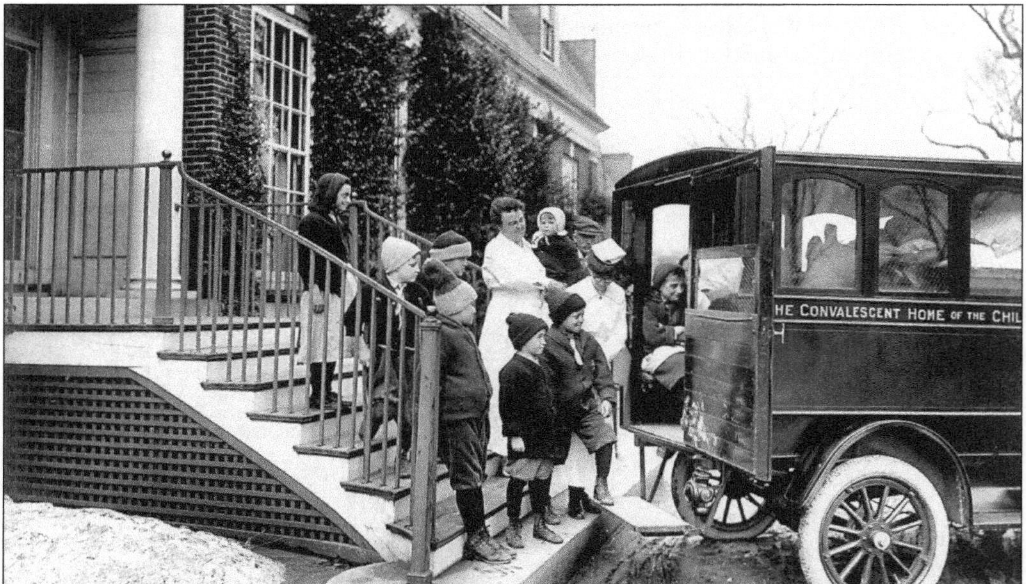

AN AMBULANCE SHUTTLE, 1920. During the 1920s and 1930s, a special ambulance shuttled patients between the Convalescent Home and Children's Hospital on Longwood Avenue. The Boston streetcar system included a special car that transported children, nurses, and doctors from Children's Hospital to the Wellesley stop once a week. There, a horse-drawn barge and later a motorized ambulance would carry them directly to the Convalescent Home.

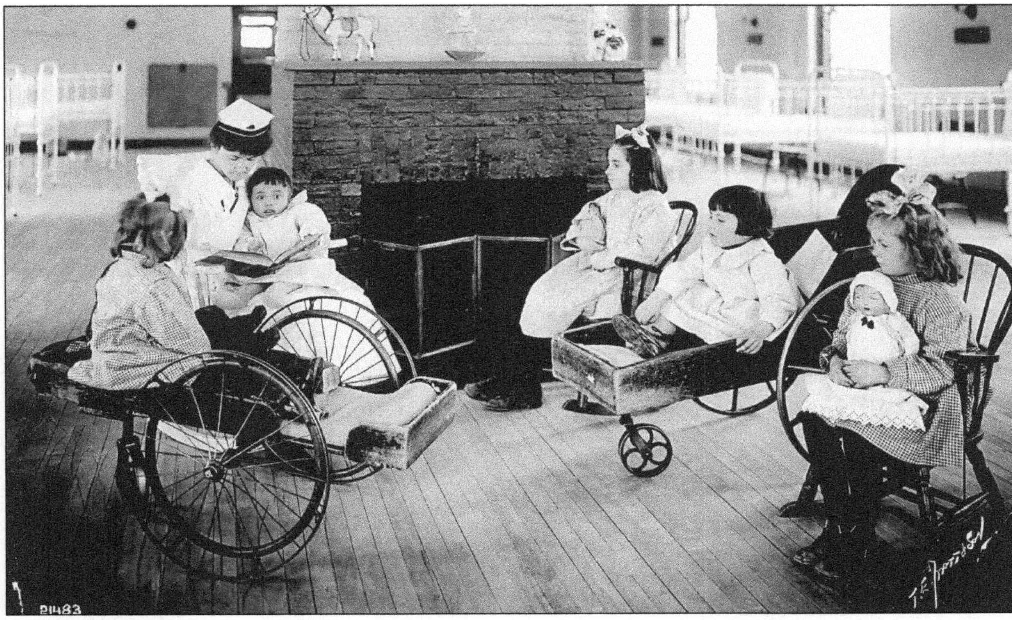

THE GIRLS' WARD, C. 1925. The large, open wards were modeled after those on Huntington Avenue and let in a great deal of sunlight and fresh air. The Convalescent Home was staffed by graduates of the Children's Hospital School of Nursing. Go-carts similar to those seen here are still in use in the hospital today.

THE GIRLS' DINING TABLE, C. 1925. Providing nutritious meals in a communal setting was an important goal of convalescent care.

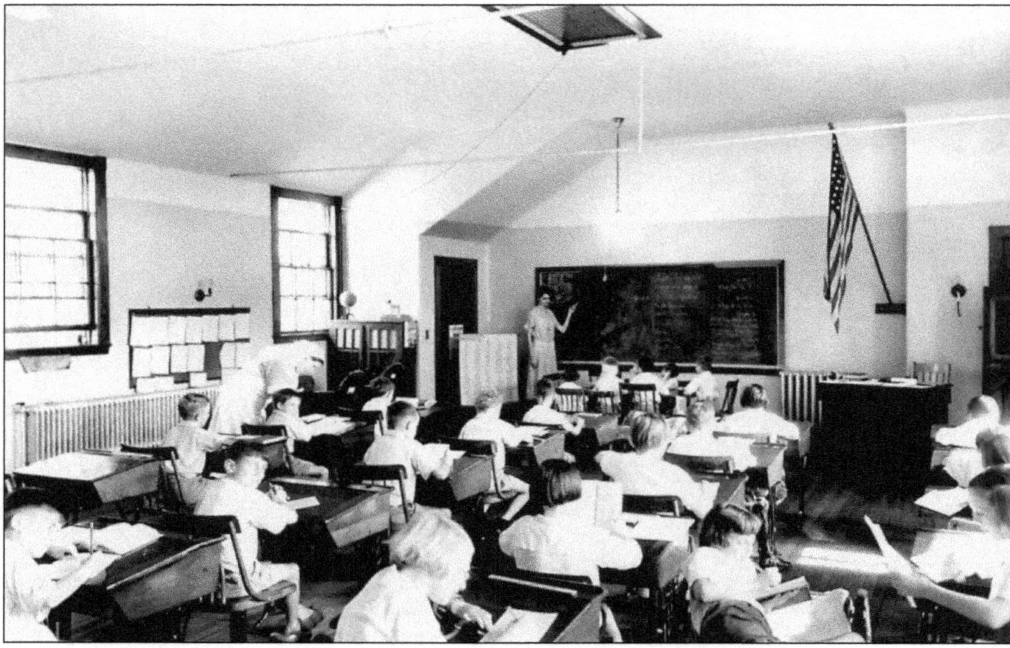

THE CLASSROOM, C. 1925. Children at the Convalescent Home received education even while patients. This was especially important because hospitalizations tended to be very lengthy. Nursing students and volunteers helped with school assignments.

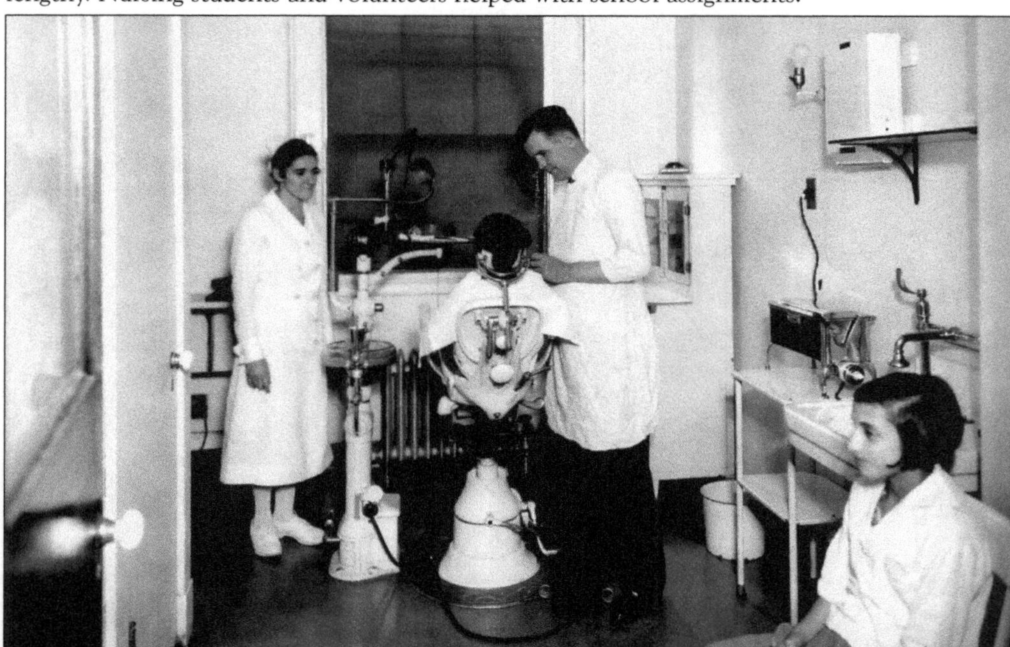

THE DENTISTS' ROOM. Over time, the Convalescent Home came to feature many of the same clinical care units as Children's Hospital. An isolation ward was opened at the home in 1926, and later, additional care services were arranged, such as the dental clinic shown here.

THE CHAPEL. The Convalescent Home, like the Nurses' Home and Children's Hospital, had a small chapel where children, their parents, and other visitors could pray and meditate.

ANNE SMITH ROBBINS. Organized by Anne Smith Robbins in 1861 on McLean Street in Boston, the House of the Good Samaritan was a home for the chronically ill, the majority of its patients women with tuberculosis. In 1863, however, children with tuberculosis were admitted as well. Institutional care for children continued here when the Wellesley Convalescent Home closed in 1958.

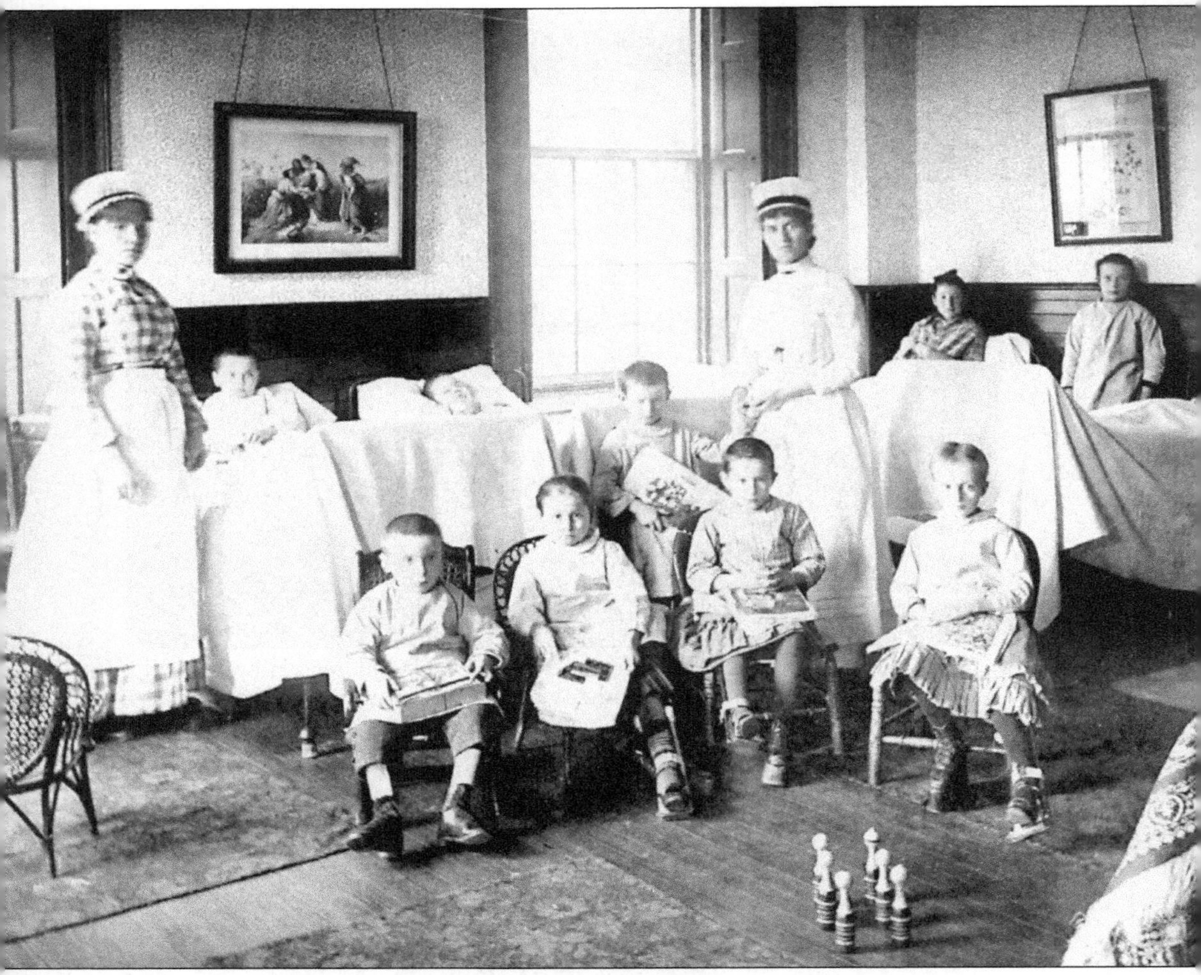

THE CHILDREN'S WARD, 1863. The House of the Good Samaritan filled a great need in providing convalescent care for children in Boston, both in the years before and after the founding of Children's Hospital in 1869. The house was attractively decorated and furnished; it provided comfort for patients ill with tubercular spinal and hip disease.

THE HOUSE OF THE GOOD SAMARITAN, 25 BINNEY STREET, C. 1906. The Good Samaritan, like Children's Hospital, outgrew its original facilities and relocated to the corner of Francis and Binney Streets in the Longwood area in 1905. Initially, 40 beds were available.

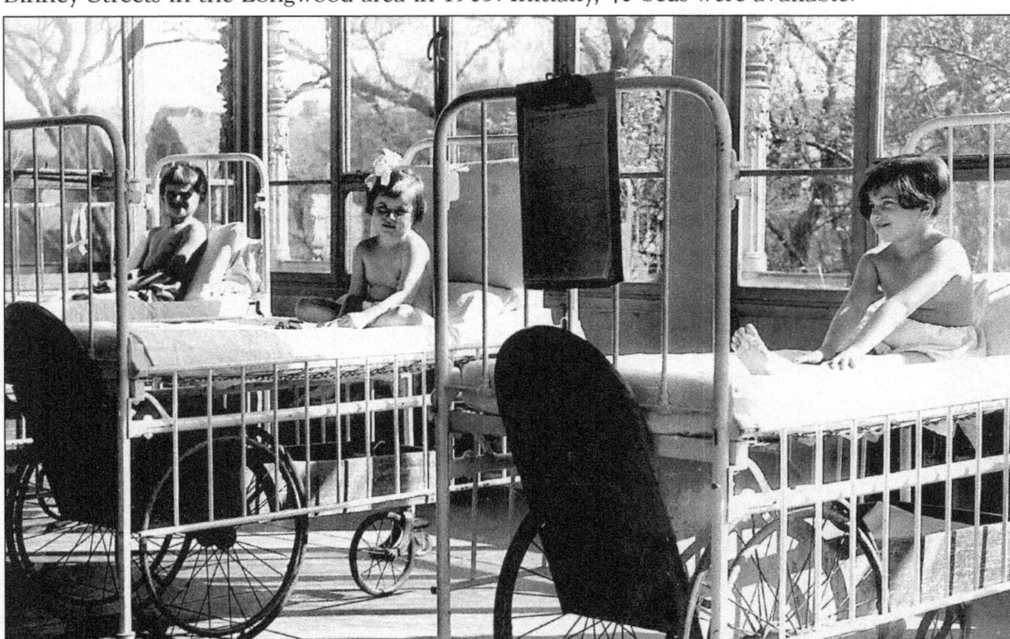

THE SUN WARD. Sunlight and fresh air were considered important treatments for tuberculosis. The Good Samaritan provided regular exposure to sunlight for its patients, such as these children. Their beds were wheeled to facilitate ease of transport and to bring patients outdoors for fresh air. Wooden go-carts can be seen parked under patient beds.

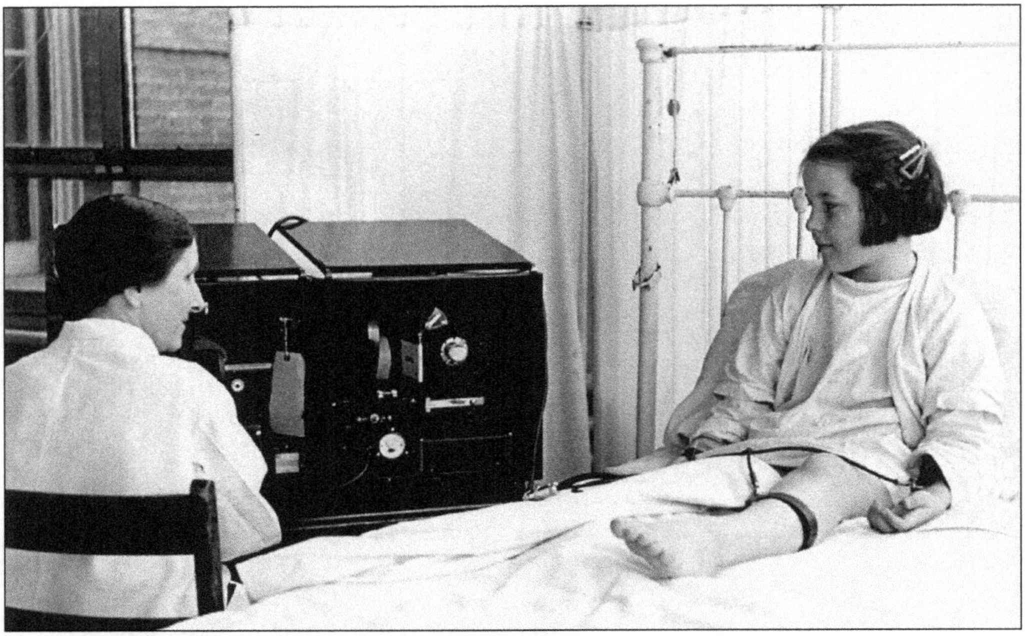

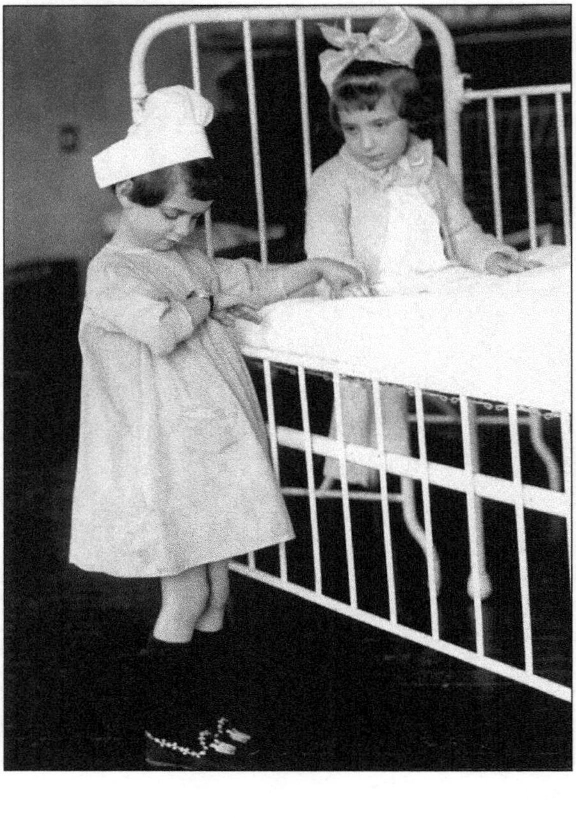

RHEUMATIC HEART DISEASE. As tuberculosis waned, the House of the Good Samaritan changed its focus to concentrate primarily on the treatment of rheumatic fever and rheumatic heart disease. An addition was built specifically for this purpose; in 1930, as many as 54 patients out of a possible 74 had rheumatic fever. Above, a child is given an electrocardiogram with a primitive device. Antibiotic therapy eventually made even this work obsolete. The House of the Good Samaritan was incorporated into the Children's Hospital Medical Center in 1958. Its site is now occupied by Brigham and Women's Hospital.

DR. VINCENT Y. BOWDITCH. In 1891, this dapper gentleman founded the Sharon Sanatorium. Bowditch observed that the town was free from tuberculosis and, believing that therefore its air was healthier than anywhere else, decided "to supply a suitable institution for the treatment of incipient pulmonary diseases, only arising in those who are unable . . . to seek distant health resorts."

THE SHARON SANATORIUM, 1915. Like the Wellesley Convalescent Home, the Sharon Sanatorium provided fresh air, good food from the facility's own garden, sunshine, regulated exercise, and rest. Treatments concentrated on air quality, and even on the coldest winter days, patients stayed outside on sleeping porches, bundled up in warm clothes and blankets. As was true for the Wellesley Convalescent Home and the House of the Good Samaritan, advances in medicine reduced admissions and the need for the sanatorium's services. In 1938, however, Children's Hospital made an arrangement to send children with a history of rheumatic fever to Sharon, marking the beginning of a long relationship. Financial difficulties finally forced the sanatorium to close in 1947.

SARAH FULLER, 1869. Sarah Fuller studied at the Clarke School for the Deaf in Northampton to prepare for a new job as the principal of Boston's Horace Mann School for Deaf-Mutes in 1869. In 1870, she learned of Alexander Melville Bell's system for teaching "visible speech" to the deaf and, in 1871, invited his son Alexander Graham Bell to teach the system in Boston. She founded the Home for Little Deaf Children in 1902.

THE HOME FOR LITTLE CHILDREN WHO CANNOT HEAR, 1907. Known as "the Oaks" in Sarah Fuller's later life, the home prepared students to enroll in the Horace Mann School for Deaf-Mutes. It closed in 1927, when many parents believed it better to educate deaf children at home. Subsequently, the Sarah Fuller Foundation for Little Deaf Children was established to provide at-home schooling. Today, the Sarah Fuller Foundation supports the Department of Otolaryngology and Communication Disorders at Children's Hospital.

Five

The Development of an International Medical Center

1946–1990

Following the end of World War II, experienced physicians returned from military service. Resources became available for peacetime application, and medical advances accelerated. Government, understanding the importance of research to the nation's health, established programs to support academic research and increased funding dramatically. With its foundation of clinical and research excellence, Children's Hospital was well positioned to take a leadership role in pediatric health, and did so.

Children's Hospital reorganized itself as the Children's Hospital Medical Center to improve coordination of the hospital's medical and surgical departments, as well as specialty care in several different fields. New buildings were necessary to support the hospital's integrated and expanding clinical, research, and educational missions. The Farley Building (1956) increased space for inpatient care. The Fegan Building (1967) provided ambulatory and outpatient clinics. The Martha Eliot Health Center (1967) reached directly into the community to bring Children's Hospital expertise to neighborhood children and adolescents. In 1970, Children's Hospital built a 13-story research building named for John Enders, a Children's Hospital scientist who, with his colleagues Frederick Robbins and Thomas Weller, had won the Nobel Prize for pioneering work with the poliovirus. In 1987, increasing demand from a now global patient base required Children's Hospital to build again, this time a new facility including additional space for inpatient care, operating rooms, and state-of-the-art imaging equipment.

Medical care in all sub-specialties flourished, often based on new discoveries from basic and clinical research. Some old diseases, such as polio and measles, decreased in prevalence because of vaccines; others, such as meningitis, decreased in morbidity because of antibiotics; and some conditions began to yield to new surgical techniques or modes of pharmacological treatment.

Still, new challenges emerged. Some, such as HIV and adolescent substance abuse, reflected new social circumstances. Others, such as many mental and communication disorders, reflected a more refined awareness and the availability of new diagnostic and therapeutic tools.

During this period, training of students, residents, and fellows continued as a central mission, as Children's Hospital educated a broad spectrum of extraordinary primary and specialist pediatric clinicians and scientists. These alumni are in many ways the hospital's greatest gift to pediatric healthcare and its greatest investment in the future of medical and biological research.

Effective leadership, strong philanthropic support, and dedicated staff and employees enabled Children's Hospital to keep pace with increasing demands on its services and challenges to its mission, and to expand that mission in the local, regional, national, and international communities.

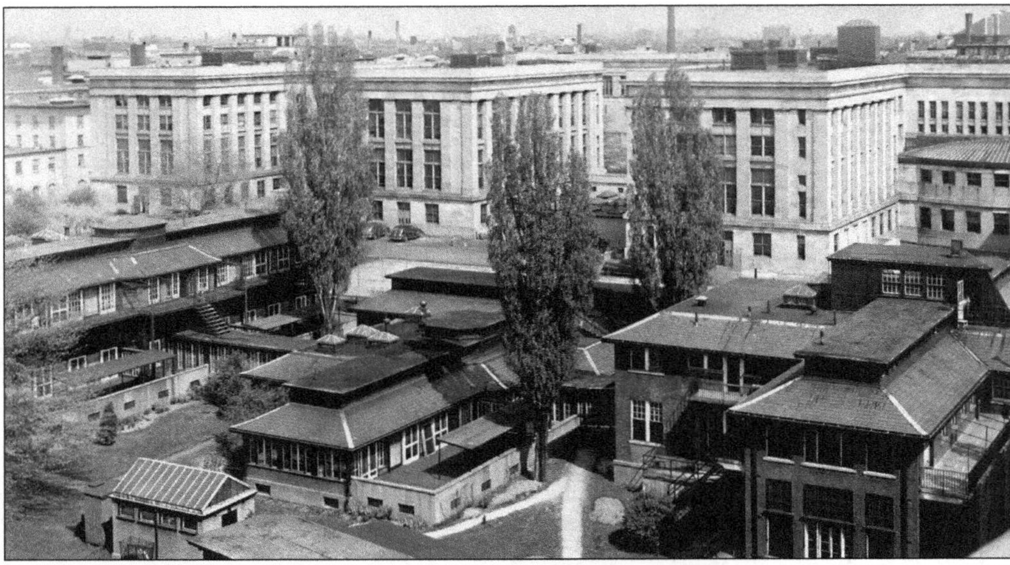

Children's Hospital Wards, 1953. With continued expansion of the hospital and the additional services made available through affiliations with the Infants' Hospital, Sharon Sanatorium, House of the Good Samaritan, and other institutions, Children's Hospital's original facilities proved to be less and less adequate. The old cottage wards (seen here in front of the larger buildings of Harvard Medical School) became antiquated as the hospital began to grow steadily from a primarily Boston-based institution to an international medical center.

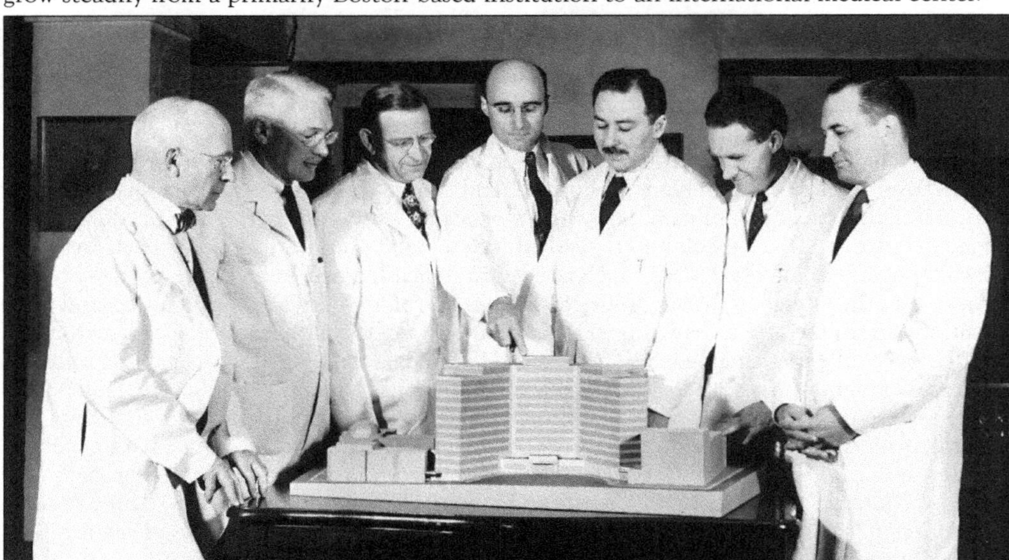

Medical Center Planners, 1946. Several department chiefs meet to plan the new medical center soon after World War II. The doctors pictured here are, from left to right, Burt Wolbach, Franc Ingraham, William Green, Guy Brugler (Children's Hospital director), Sidney Farber, Charles Janeway, and Robert Gross. Dr. Leonard Cronkite, general director and president from 1962 to 1977, saw the medical center plan to its completion. He was ably assisted by Dr. Lendon Snedeker, administrator and author of the book *One Hundred Years at Children's*.

"LITTLE MIKE" FARLEY, HOSPITAL PRESIDENT, 1948. The financial driving force for the medical center was hospital president John Wells Farley. Under his administration, the hospital achieved remarkable growth in services and facilities. In 1956, a new building for inpatient care was named after him.

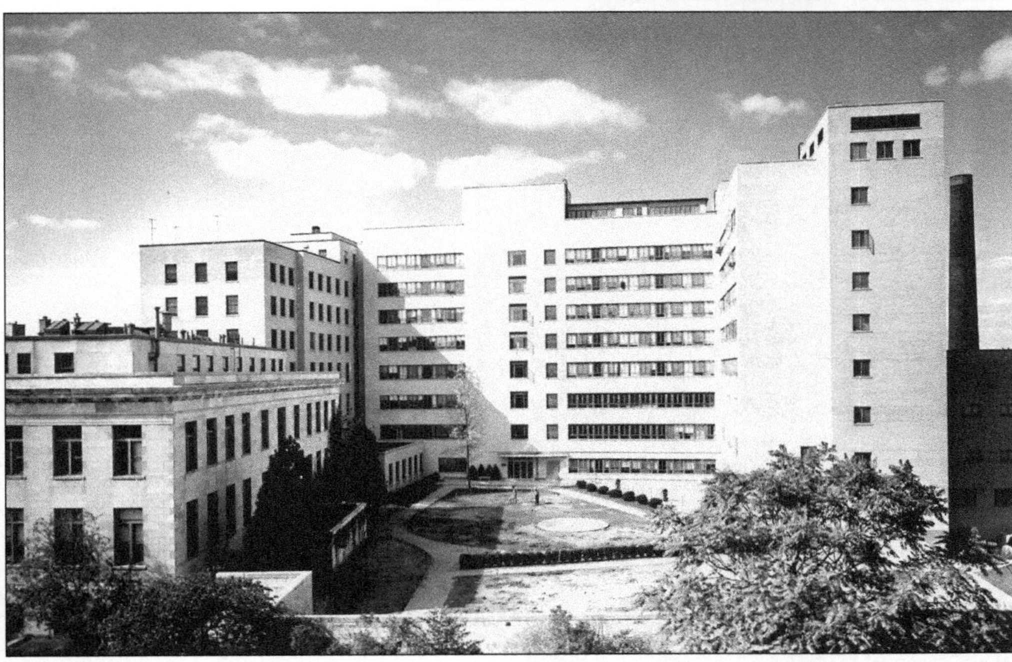

THE CHILDREN'S HOSPITAL MEDICAL CENTER CAMPUS, 1955. The medical center soon became a model for hospital expansion throughout the country. The new buildings, on the site of the old cottage wards, surrounded a central open space that soon became the Prouty Garden. The Fegan Building for outpatients was completed in 1967.

THE PROUTY GARDEN. Olive Higgins Prouty, a well-known American novelist and Children's Hospital benefactor, and her husband gave an endowment for a garden named in their daughters' honor. Designed by the landscape architectural firm of Olmsted Brothers (who also planned Central Park in New York City and the Emerald Necklace in Boston), the Prouty Garden opened in 1956. Here, Olive Prouty watches as a young boy plants a tree, with assistance from hospital president William Wolbach and another patient.

THE PROUTY GARDEN, C. 1980. Thanks to the Prouty family's vision, generosity, and love of children, this garden lives on at Children's Hospital as a gift to patients, families, and visitors who enjoy its open space, beauty, and serenity. The garden remains a relaxing, green space amid the buildings now occupying almost all of the once open land around the hospital.

THE STATUE UNVEILING, 1989. To celebrate the 100th anniversary of the founding of the Children's Hospital School of Nursing—and, ironically, the 10th anniversary of its closing—the hospital and the School of Nursing Alumnae Association dedicated this statue of a student nurse walking hand in hand with a young patient. David Weiner, Children's Hospital president from 1979 to 2000, and Linda S. Cornell, RN, unveiled the statue, which is modeled after the photograph on the cover of this book. The statue is located in the Prouty Garden.

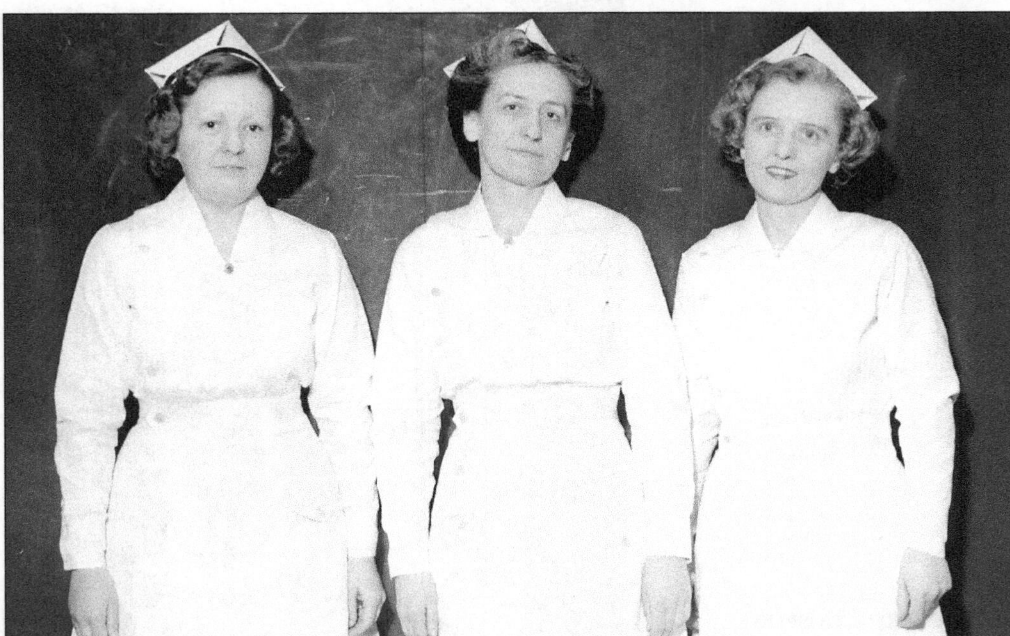

MURIEL VESEY, RN. Vesey, appearing here with other senior nurses (assistant director Phyllis Downing, RN, left, and associate director Theresa Hurley, RN), served as director of nursing and the School of Nursing from 1946 to 1973. A dignified, soft-spoken leader with a subtle sense of humor, she was the consummate clinical administrator of Children's Hospital.

A Haven for Patients. Through the years, nursing care has changed dramatically at Children's Hospital and in hospitals worldwide. Formal education and technological innovation are central to the discipline of nursing, but not a substitute for the loving care of nurses and the bonds they form with their young patients.

Entering the Hospital, c. 1950. A mother and child arrive at Children's Hospital. Both literally and symbolically, they are entering a new era of pediatric medical care in Boston.

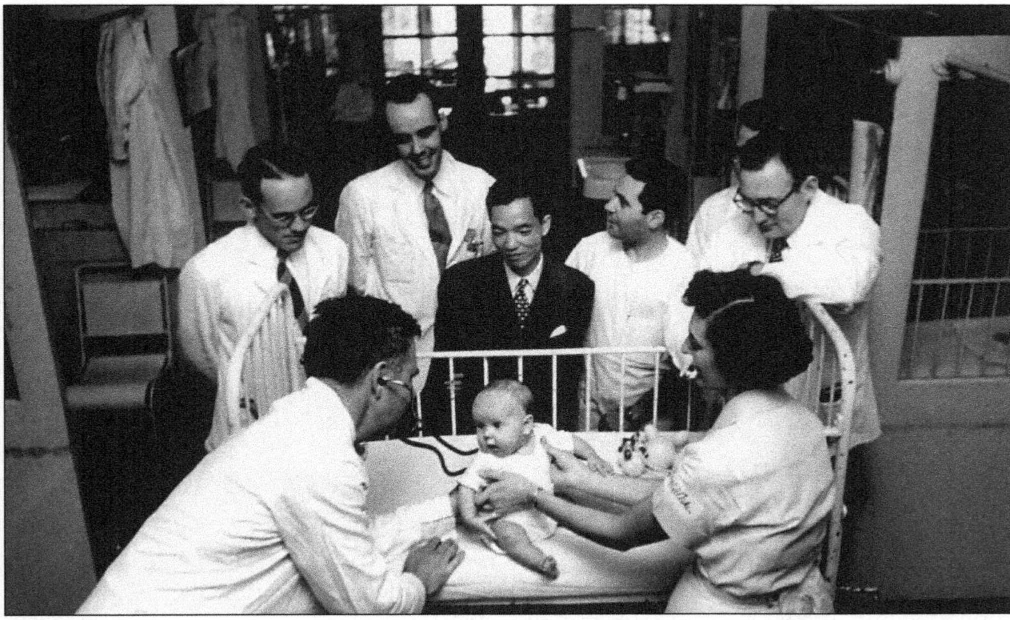

DR. CLEMENT A. SMITH, C. 1950. Dr. Clement A. Smith (front left) was one of the first full-time pediatricians to concentrate on newborns. He helped develop the new field of neonatology with his research on prematurity and newborn physiology. A prolific author, he wrote *The Children's Hospital of Boston: "Built Better Than They Knew"* (1983), a comprehensive history of the institution. Here, Smith makes his rounds accompanied by house staff and a visitor.

DR. CHARLES A. JANEWAY, C. 1970. One of the most significant figures in pediatric history, Dr. Charles Janeway was physician in chief from 1946 to 1974, the longest term in the history of the hospital. A renowned scientist, he was central to the development of sub-specialties within the Department of Medicine. He trained countless pediatricians, many of whom assumed leadership positions in the United States and abroad. He was a revered figure in national and international pediatrics.

DR. CHARLES JANEWAY'S MEDICAL HOUSE STAFF AND FACULTY, 1949. Janeway's house staff reflected the growth and sophistication of graduate medical education after World War II. During the war, women were accepted as house officers, taking over for those male physicians who had entered military service. The first woman to serve as chief resident was Dr. Gretchen Hutchins in 1946, the year Janeway became physician in chief.

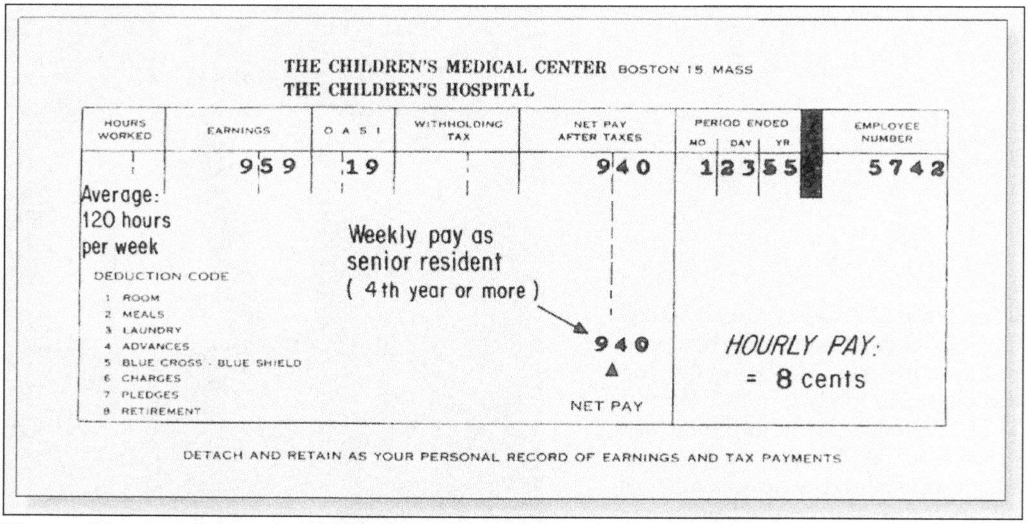

THE CHILDREN'S MEDICAL CENTER BOSTON 15 MASS
THE CHILDREN'S HOSPITAL

HOURS WORKED	EARNINGS	O A S I	WITHHOLDING TAX	NET PAY AFTER TAXES	PERIOD ENDED MO | DAY | YR	EMPLOYEE NUMBER
	9 59	19		9 40	12 3 55	5742

Average:
120 hours
per week

Weekly pay as
senior resident
(4th year or more)

DEDUCTION CODE
1 ROOM
2 MEALS
3 LAUNDRY
4 ADVANCES
5 BLUE CROSS - BLUE SHIELD
6 CHARGES
7 PLEDGES
8 RETIREMENT

940
NET PAY

HOURLY PAY:
= 8 cents

DETACH AND RETAIN AS YOUR PERSONAL RECORD OF EARNINGS AND TAX PAYMENTS

HOUSE OFFICER COMPENSATION, 1955. This paycheck was issued in 1955 to a senior resident in surgery at Children's Hospital. The salary was less than $10 per week, which came out to 8¢ per hour, considering that duty in the hospital was every other night and weekend. Although house officers still work very hard, their hospital activities are limited to 80 hours per week, and they receive a better salary.

Dr. Mary Ellen Avery with Dr. Charles Janeway, 1974. Janeway's successor was Dr. Mary Ellen Avery, one of the first women to lead an academic department at Harvard Medical School. In 1959, she first described surfactant deficiency as a cause of hyaline membrane disease. Since surfactant's use in treatment, deaths from that disease have decreased by 30 percent worldwide. Avery established the Joint Program in Neonatology at Children's, Beth Israel, and Peter Bent Brigham Hospitals. She received the National Medal of Science and was the first pediatrician to chair the American Association for the Advancement of Science.

Avery's Medical House Staff, 1983. When Avery succeeded Janeway in 1974, 53 resident physicians were serving as house officers. Of these, the vast majority were men. By 1990, the staff had grown to 82 resident physicians, more than half of whom were women.

THE ADOLESCENT UNIT, 1970. In 1954, Dr. J. Roswell Gallagher (left) established the Adolescent Unit at Children's Hospital, which provided clinical care, emotional support, and referrals to appropriate sub-specialists. Dr. Robert Masland (right) assumed leadership in 1967, when Gallagher retired.

DR. LOUIS K. DIAMOND AND THE BLOOD GROUPING LABORATORY. Dr. Louis Diamond (far right) devoted his professional career to Children's Hospital, starting as a house officer under Dr. Kenneth Blackfan and advancing to chief resident, faculty member, and ultimately, chief of hematology. Diamond described *erythroblastosis fetalis*, a devastating blood disorder in newborns, and the process of exchange transfusion by which the disease could be treated. Along with Dr. Charles Janeway, he founded the Blood Grouping Laboratory at Children's Hospital, a unit that led to advances in hematology, immunology, and genetics. This laboratory later became the Center for Blood Research at Harvard Medical School.

Dr. Sidney Farber, c. 1950. Dr. Sidney Farber was the successor to Dr. S. Burt Wolbach, chief of pathology. He and his staff developed the first effective treatment for childhood leukemia, which began the use of chemotherapy for cancer. Farber was instrumental in developing the Children's Hospital Medical Center in the 1940s and 1950s. He also served as a leader in the establishment of the Children's Cancer Research Foundation, which later became the Dana-Farber Cancer Institute.

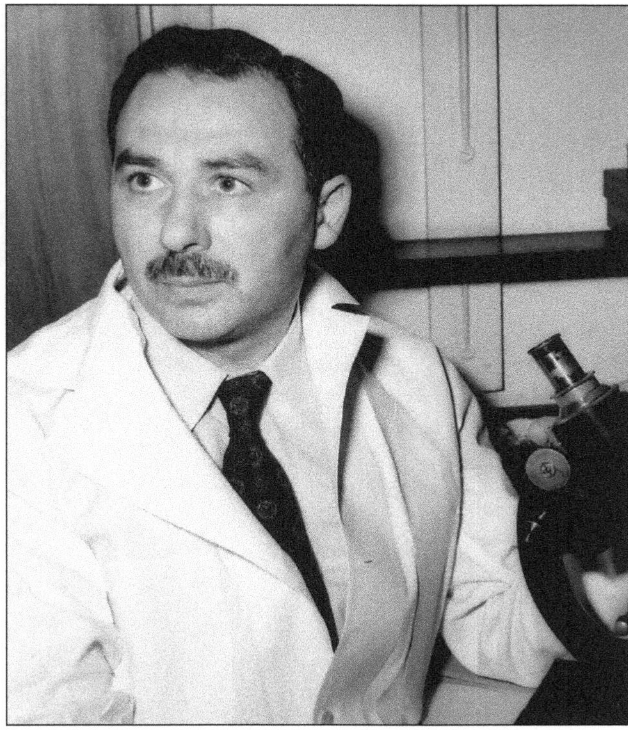

Dr. David Nathan, c. 1980. Dr. David Nathan was chief of hematology and oncology from 1968 to 1985, replacing Diamond. Then appointed physician in chief at Children's Hospital, he served until 1995, when he became president of the Dana-Farber Cancer Institute. Along with Dr. Frank Oski and Dr. Stuart Orkin, he wrote *Hematology of Infancy and Children*, a text that remains a classic in its field.

GENETICS AND IMMUNOLOGY. Following training at Children's with Dr. Louis Diamond and a year abroad studying genetics, Dr. Park Gerald (right) was appointed chief of the newly organized Division of Clinical Genetics in 1965. He helped to describe the structure of hemoglobin and several abnormal hemoglobin molecules. Dr. Fred Rosen (left), who interned under Dr. Sidney Farber in pathology, established the Immunology Research Laboratory in 1959 and became chief of immunology in 1968. He was appointed the first James L. Gamble Professor of Pediatrics in 1972 and, later, president of the Center for Blood Research at Harvard Medical School.

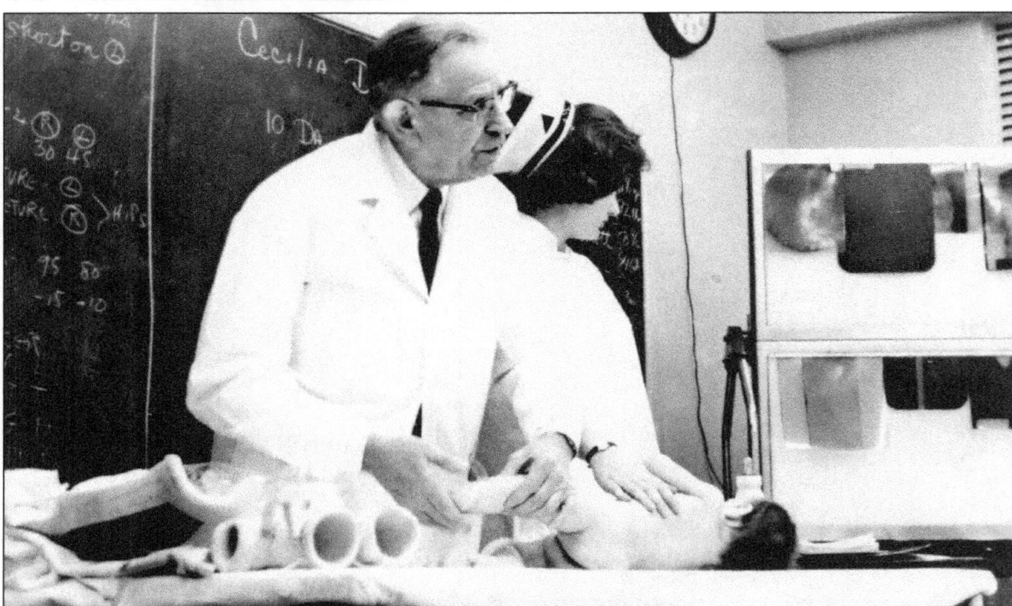

DR. WILLIAM GREEN, CHIEF OF ORTHOPEDIC SURGERY, C. 1960. Dr. William Green served as chief of the Department of Orthopedic Surgery from 1946 to 1968. Director of the Massachusetts Infantile Paralysis Clinics at Children's Hospital, he also pioneered many advances for the care of polio patients. In 1962, he was appointed the Harriett M. Peabody Professor of Pediatric Orthopedic Surgery at Harvard Medical School.

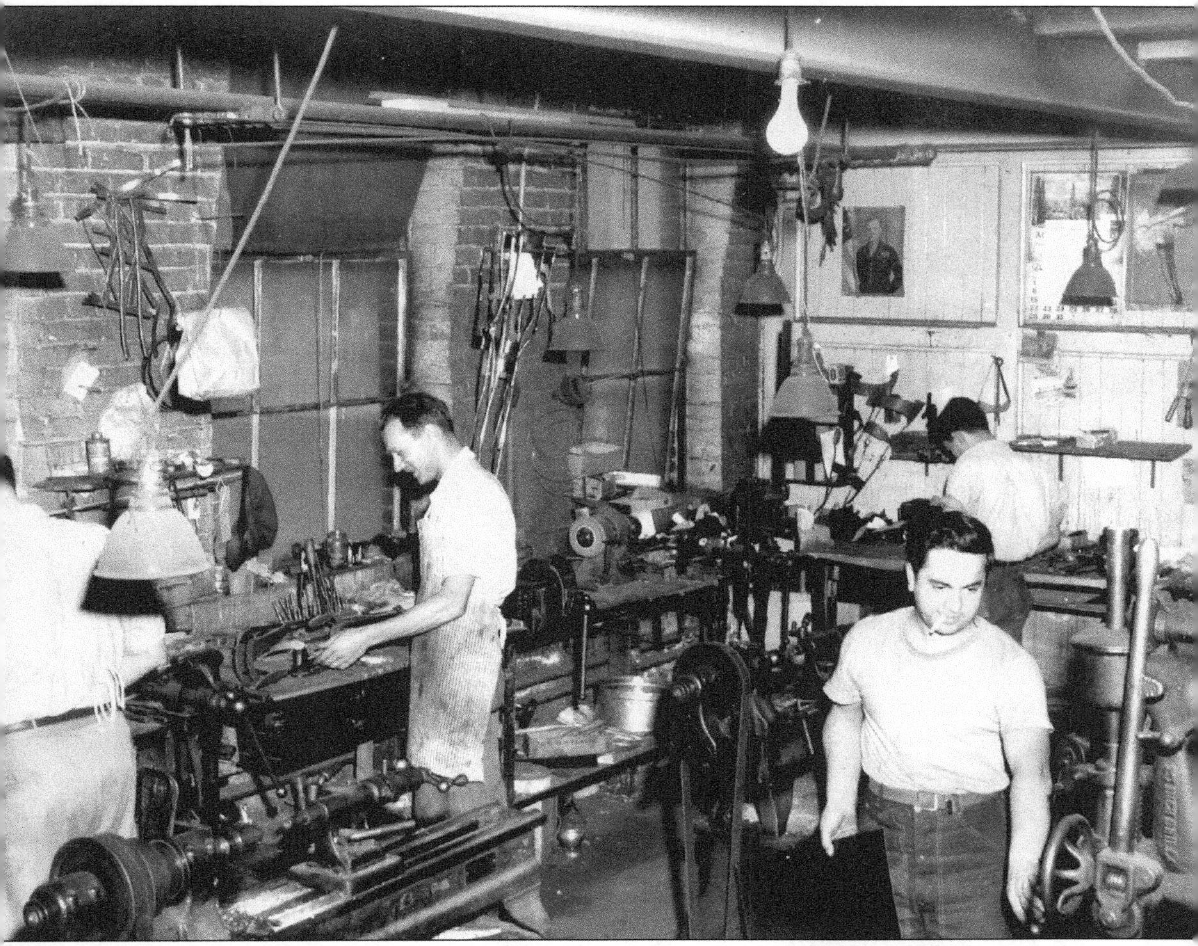

THE ORTHOPEDIC BRACE SHOP. Originally known as the Charitable Surgical Appliance Shop, the Orthopedic Brace Shop was established in 1884. Since then, it has fashioned and repaired appliances needed to treat children with bone, muscle, and nerve disorders. It now serves the Boston medical community as one branch of the National Orthotics and Prosthetics Company.

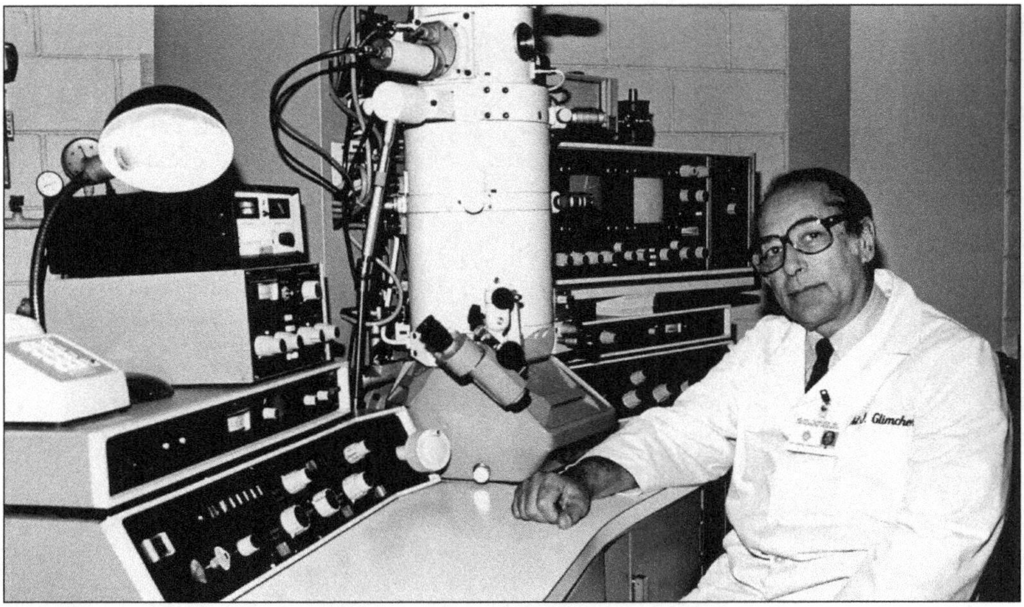

DR. MELVIN GLIMCHER, ORTHOPEDIC RESEARCH. Dr. Melvin Glimcher came to Children's Hospital in 1970 as the Peabody Professor of Pediatric Orthopedic Surgery. His focus was in orthopedic research. Glimcher established a major research laboratory in the Department of Orthopedics to explore the structure, physiology, and biochemistry of bone.

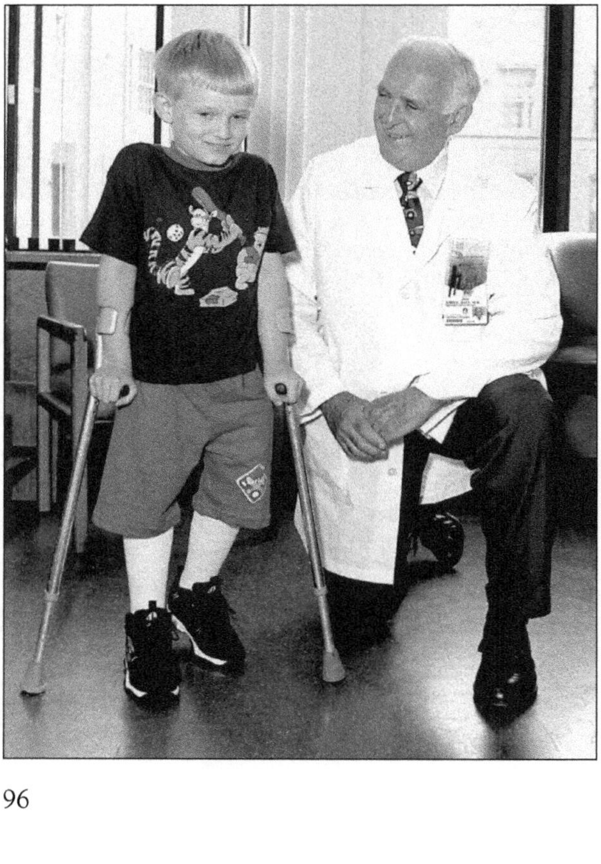

DR. JOHN HALL, 1997. After beginning his career at the Hospital for Sick Children in Toronto, Dr. John Hall became chairman of the Department of Orthopedic Surgery at Children's Hospital. As tuberculosis and polio became rare, he focused on orthopedic anomalies in children, especially scoliosis. He was one of the developers of the "Boston brace."

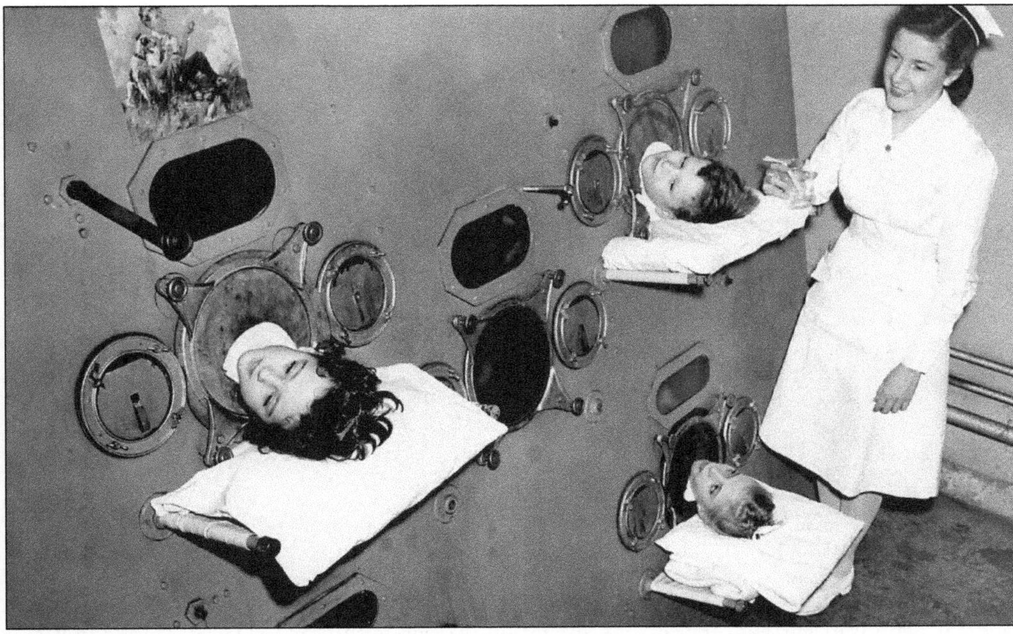

The Exterior of an Iron Lung, Early 1950s. These room-sized respirators were in nearly continuous use for the treatment of respiratory failure caused by polio during epidemics in the early 1950s. Progress in virology eventually rendered these huge machines obsolete.

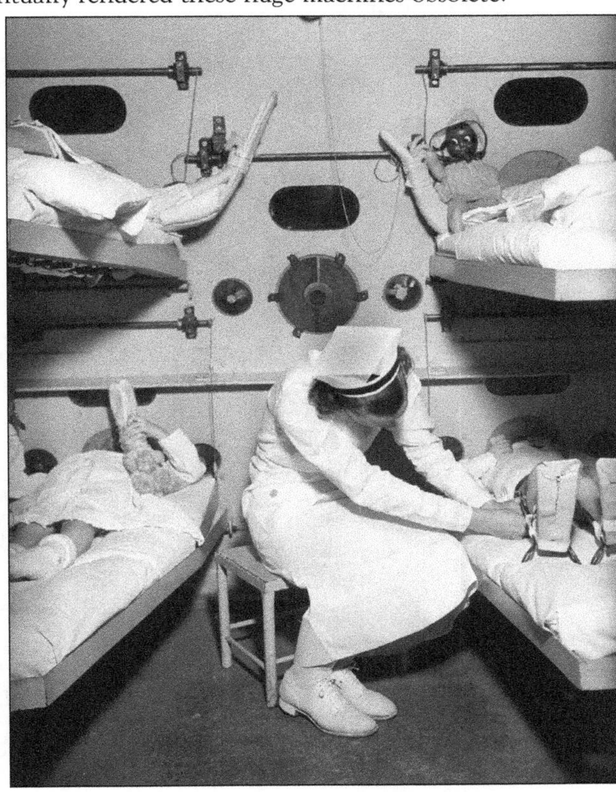

The Interior of an Iron Lung, Early 1950s. Here, a nurse adjusts braces for a patient inside a respirator. (Courtesy Harvard Medical Library.)

Dr. John F. Enders and Polio. What Dr. Louis Diamond was to hematology and Dr. Sidney Farber to cancer, Dr. John Enders was to virology research and poliomyelitis, an epidemic scourge of the 20th century. He spent more than 20 years at Children's Hospital and Harvard Medical School in various laboratories, including this laboratory of Dr. Hans Zinsser in 1927. Enders, along with associates Dr. Frederick Robbins and Dr. Thomas Weller, former Children's Hospital pediatric house officers, first cultivated the poliovirus in the late 1940s. (Courtesy Harvard Medical Library.)

Enders and the Nobel Prize. Enders, Robbins, and Weller shared the Nobel Prize for Medicine in 1954 for their landmark research on the poliovirus performed in Children's Hospital research laboratories. This achievement soon led to the development of vaccines to prevent the potentially devastating effects of polio and other viral diseases.

Dr. John F. Enders and Dr. Mary Ellen Avery, 1981. Taken in a relaxed moment in the Prouty Garden four years before Dr. John Enders's death, this photograph serves as a reminder of the close relationship between pediatric research and clinical care, an interdependence that Children's Hospital strives to perpetuate. Mary Bunting Smith, emeritus president of Radcliffe College, is visible in the background.

The Enders Research Building. In 1970, this new research facility was named in honor of Enders for his pioneering work with polio, measles, and other major viral pathogens. At the time, it was the largest facility in the world dedicated to pediatric research and represented a major commitment of Children's Hospital to basic scientific investigation. An addition in 1990 doubled the size of the Enders Building and enabled more than 1,000 research staff members to work within its walls.

The Department of Neurosurgery, c. 1960. Dr. Franc Ingraham, chairman of the department (first row, right), and his protégé and successor, Dr. Donald Matson (first row, left), co-authored the landmark textbook *Neurosurgery of Infancy and Childhood* in 1954. They pioneered the development of effective treatments for many complex brain conditions affecting children, including subdural hematoma, craniosynostosis, and hydrocephalus.

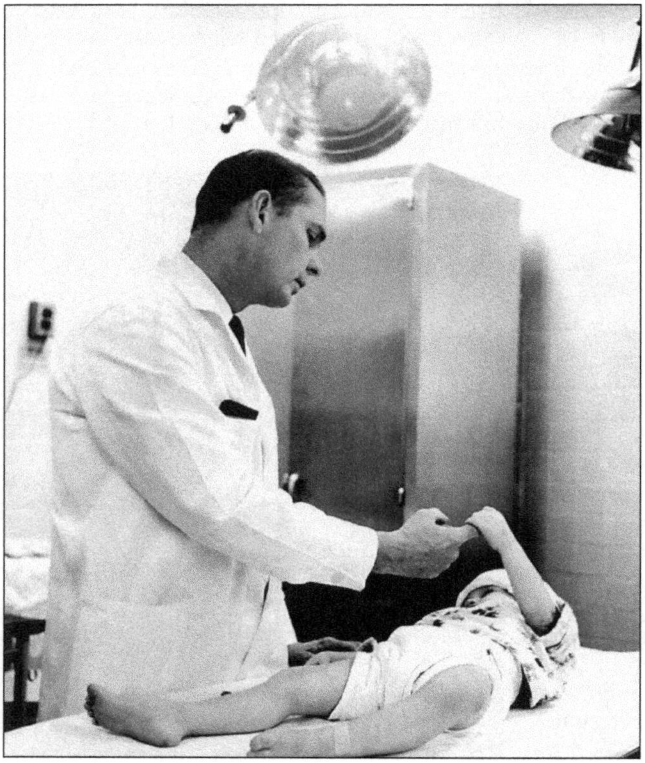

Dr. Donald Matson with a Patient, 1960. After working with Dr. Franc Ingraham for many years, Dr. Donald Matson succeeded him as neurosurgeon in chief. In 1968, he was appointed the first Franc Douglas Ingraham Professor of Neurosurgery at Harvard Medical School. His untimely death in 1969 at the age of 55 resulted from a progressive central nervous system disease acquired from a patient with a transmittable viral illness.

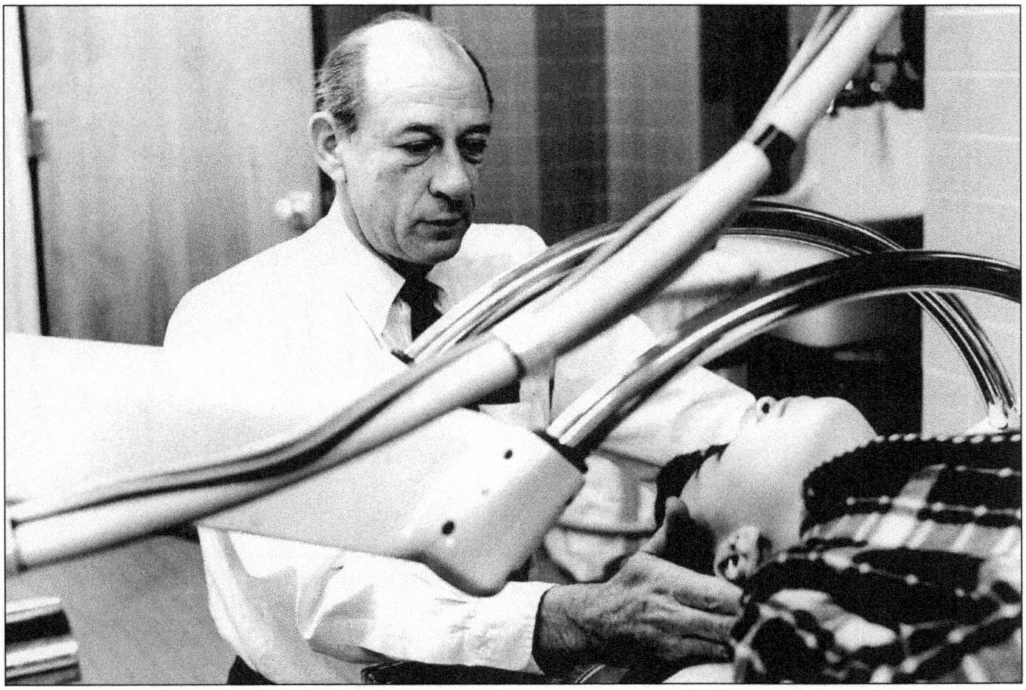

Dr. Edward Neuhauser and Radiology, 1964. Considered to be a useful service, radiology became indispensable to the immense advances occurring in pediatric medicine and surgery. Dr. Edward Neuhauser, seen here positioning a patient for an x-ray, was chief of radiology from 1941 to 1974. Trained as an orthopedist, he was renowned for his encyclopedic knowledge of orthopedics and radiology.

Dr. John Kirkpatrick, c. 1980. Dr. John Kirkpatrick succeeded Neuhauser as chairman of the Radiology Department. A physician with a prodigious memory and vast knowledge of general pediatrics as well as radiology, he fostered sub-specialization in his department, including new divisions of uroradiology, neuroradiology, nuclear medicine, and ultrasonography. Known as much for his wit as his teaching skills, he is shown here in his office adjacent to the department's x-ray reading room, still a central gathering place for physicians seeking advice regarding interpretation of radiographs.

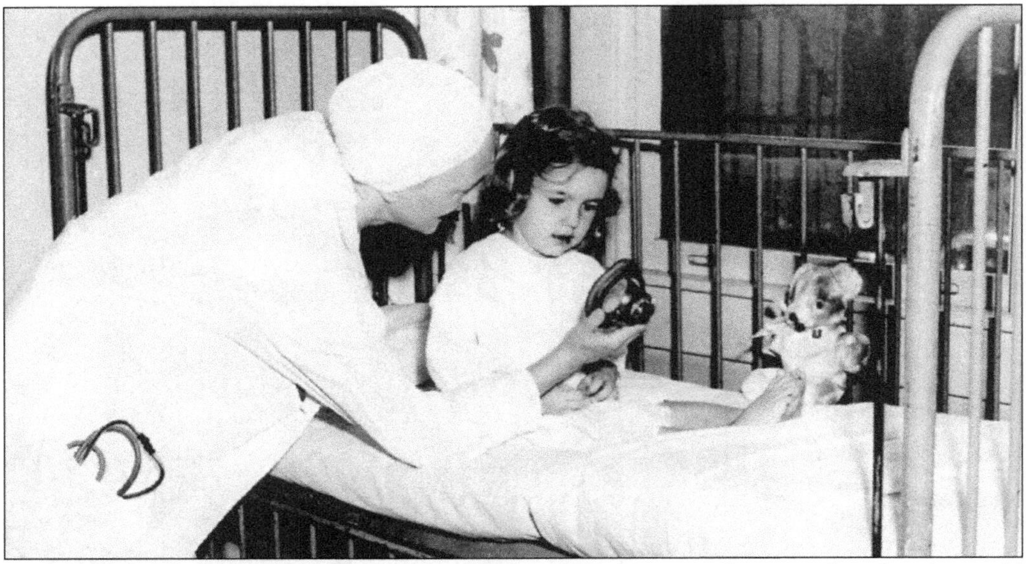

Anesthesia for Surgery, c. 1950. Decades after anesthesia was first introduced to the world in 1846 at Massachusetts General Hospital, its administration was still generally relegated to a medical student or house officer. Great skill was needed, however, to avoid potentially disastrous complications. By the 1930s, specially trained nurses at Children's Hospital were assigned to provide anesthesia for the majority of patients. Shown here is Betty Lank, RN, chief nurse anesthetist from 1935 to 1969.

Dr. Robert M. Smith and Pediatric Anesthesiology, c. 1970. Dr. Robert Smith (left, with Dr. Robert Gross) was anesthesiologist in chief from 1946 to 1980. He pioneered the development of anesthetic techniques, enabling surgeons to perform increasingly complex procedures on young patients. In addition, he established the Division of Respiratory Therapy to help care for children following surgery and trained hundreds of anesthesiologists from around the world. His textbook *Anesthesia for Infants and Children* was published in 1959.

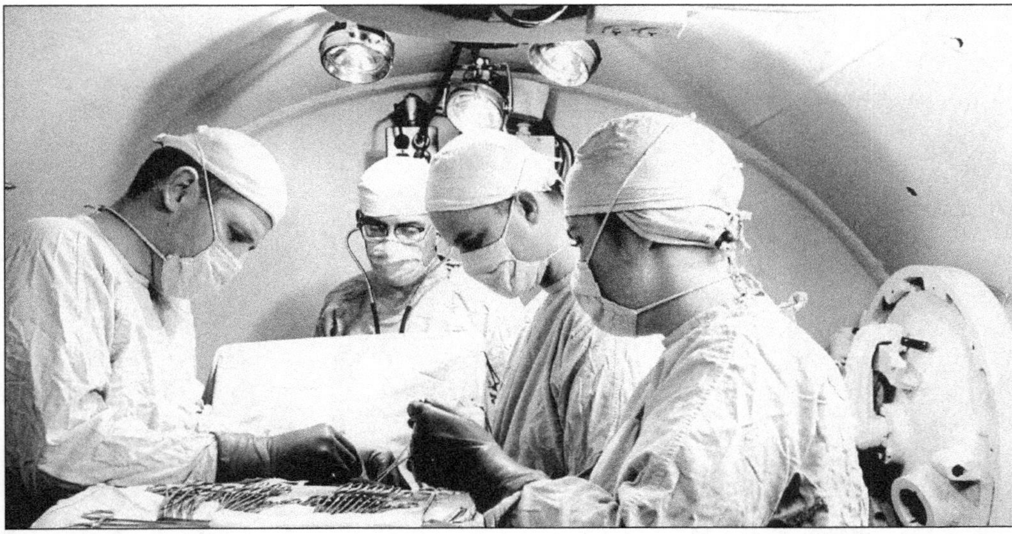

MENDING THE HEART, C. 1965. After Dr. Robert Gross demonstrated that cardiac surgery was feasible, he and other surgeons began trying to repair more complex forms of congenital heart disease. Providing sufficient oxygen to patients during these procedures, however, continued to be a major challenge. Shown here is the hyperbaric chamber used to facilitate cardiac operations at Children's Hospital for more than 200 babies in 1965, its first year of use. The subsequent development of cardiopulmonary bypass machines rendered hyperbaric chambers obsolete for this purpose.

DR. ALDO CASTANEDA AND CARDIOVASCULAR SURGERY. In 1972, Dr. Aldo Castaneda (left) succeeded Gross (right) as the William E. Ladd Professor and became chief of the Department of Cardiovascular Surgery. He helped pioneer a movement away from limited, palliative procedures for congenital heart disease to complete repairs in infancy, an approach that has led to significant improvements in long-term outcome.

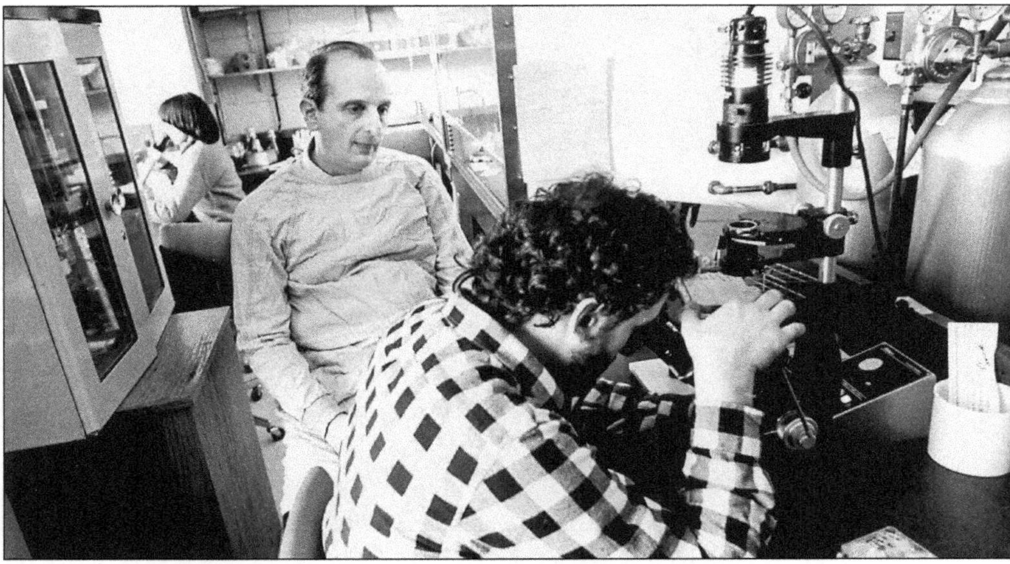

Dr. M. Judah Folkman and Surgical Research. Dr. M. Judah Folkman was appointed surgeon in chief in 1967 but relinquished this post in 1982 to devote himself fully to research in the field he pioneered, angiogenesis, the growth of new blood vessels. His groundbreaking work has led to advances in treatment for many different conditions, including cancer. He became the first incumbent of the Julia Dyckman Andrus Chair of Child Surgery at Harvard Medical School.

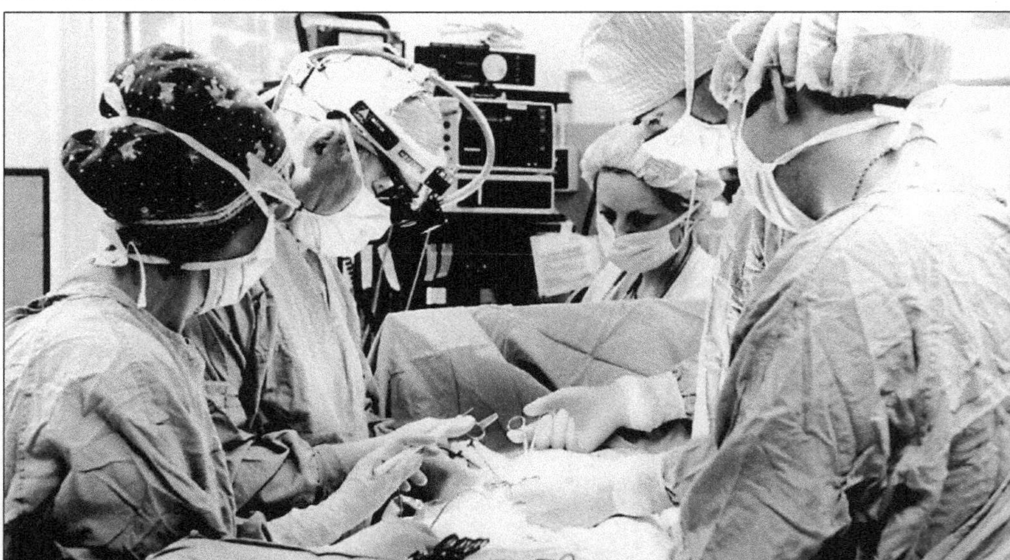

Dr. W. Hardy Hendren and Pediatric Surgery. In 1982, Dr. W. Hardy Hendren (second from left) became chief of surgery at Children's Hospital and the first incumbent of the chair in pediatric surgery at Harvard Medical School named in honor of his mentor, Dr. Robert E. Gross. Hendren pioneered major developments in pediatric urology, as well as procedures to separate conjoined twins. On his right is Dorothy Enos, RN, a Children's Hospital Nursing School graduate who assisted Hendren in the operating room for 40 years.

DR. JOSEPH MURRAY AND THE NOBEL PRIZE, 1990. Before becoming chief of plastic surgery at Children's Hospital, Dr. Joseph Murray (left) was a staff surgeon at the adjacent Peter Bent Brigham Hospital. There, in 1954, he performed the world's first successful kidney transplantation between identical twins; he continued to make contributions to the field of organ transplantation. For this work, Murray received the Nobel Prize in Medicine. Here he is accepting his award from the King of Sweden (right) in 1990.

DR. ALEXANDER NADAS AND PEDIATRIC CARDIOLOGY. Dr. Alexander Nadas came to Children's in 1949 from Hungary, becoming chief of the new Department of Cardiology in 1969. During his tenure, he oversaw the incorporation of the former Sharon Sanatorium into the medical center in 1956 and the establishment of the Cardiac Catheterization Laboratory. Nadas worked closely with cardiac surgeons to provide the physiological data needed for the care of children undergoing open-heart surgery. He trained numerous leaders in pediatric cardiology and wrote the classic text in the field.

DR. HARRY SHWACHMAN AND CYSTIC FIBROSIS. Dr. Harry Shwachman began as a house officer under Dr. Kenneth Blackfan in 1939 and served as a research fellow in pathology. He devoted his professional life to syndromes of pancreatic fibrosis, work that led to the recognition of the disease now known as cystic fibrosis. This resulted in a variety of nutritional and pulmonary treatments for the disorder. In the laboratories established by Shwachman at the Ina Sue Perlmutter Cystic Fibrosis Center, research continues.

DR. JOHN CRIGLER AND ENDOCRINOLOGY. Dr. John Crigler, founder and director of the Division of Endocrinology and the Endocrine Clinical Laboratory at Children's Hospital, was also the first director of the Clinical Research Center. He studied disorders of metabolism, including glycogen storage disease, and described a defect in bilirubin metabolism that became known as the Crigler-Najjar Syndrome.

DR. CHARLES BARLOW AND PEDIATRIC NEUROLOGY. Dr. Charles Barlow was the second incumbent of the Bronson Crothers Chair in Neurology at Harvard Medical School. Appointed neurologist in chief in 1963, he built a highly successful pediatric neurology service at Children's Hospital. His research focused on the blood-brain barrier and cerebrospinal fluid dynamics. He established one of the mental health research centers of the National Institutes of Health at Children's Hospital.

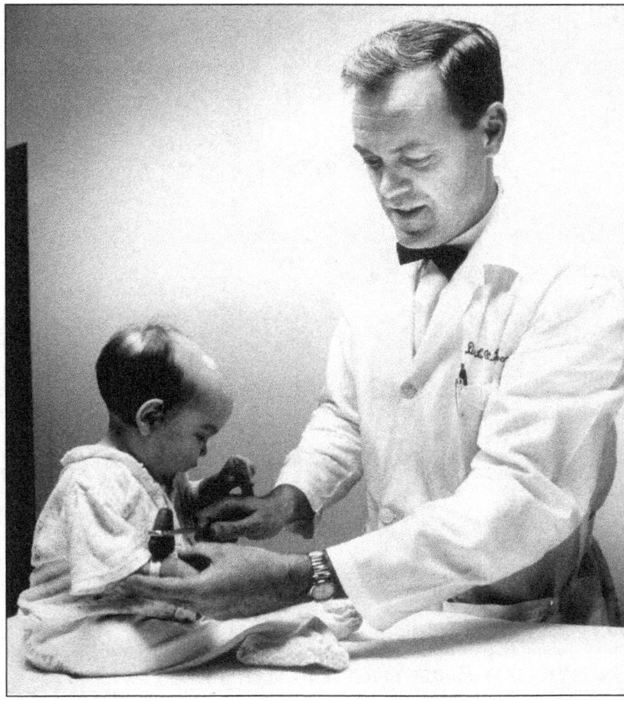

DR. JULIUS RICHMOND AND PEDIATRIC PSYCHIATRY. A pediatrician and psychiatrist by training, Dr. Julius Richmond was the director of Project Head Start during Pres. Lyndon B. Johnson's administration. He became psychiatrist in chief at Children's Hospital in 1971 and expanded the services of the Judge Baker Children's Center, founded in 1917 for abused and delinquent children and teenagers. In 1977, Richmond was appointed U.S. surgeon general and assistant secretary for health in the Department of Health, Education, and Welfare.

DR. WILLIAM BERENBERG AND CEREBRAL PALSY, 1990. Dr. William Berenberg (right) had a long, distinguished career at Children's Hospital. A resident under Dr. Kenneth Blackfan and chief resident in 1944, he went on to oversee the house officer training program, as well as the hospital's inpatient medical services. In the 1950s, he led a multi-disciplinary investigation into cerebral palsy. Dr. Frederick H. Lovejoy Jr. (left) served for four years as Dr. Charles Janeway's last chief resident and is the longtime director of the Residency Training Program in the Department of Medicine at Children's Hospital. A founder of the Massachusetts Poison Control System, he was appointed the first William Berenberg Professor of Pediatrics at Harvard Medical School.

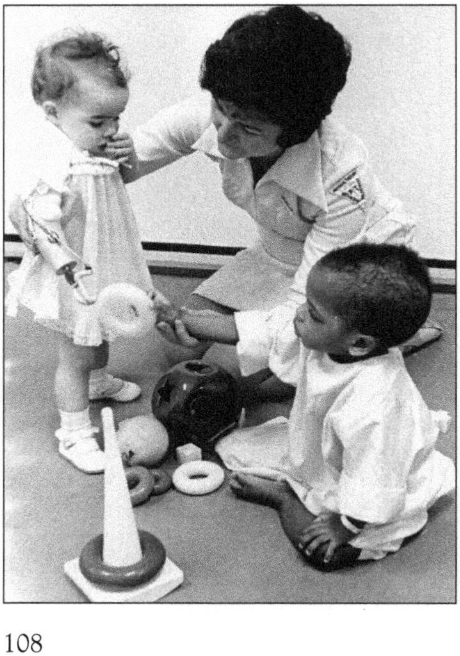

CLAIRE MCCARTHY AND PHYSICAL THERAPY, C. 1970. Physical therapists have been central to the care of children with disabilities. Here, Claire McCarthy, who became chief of physical therapy and has worked at Children's Hospital for more than 50 years, teaches a young patient to use a prosthetic arm.

ANNE BLACK, RN, AND ADVANCES IN NURSING PRACTICE. Between 1975 and 1988, new technology changed the profession dramatically. Anne Black, a visionary leader, guided the nursing program at Children's Hospital through this period of rapid evolution. As vice president of nursing, she formulated a national model for collaborative practice, interdisciplinary communication, and shared governance in nursing practice.

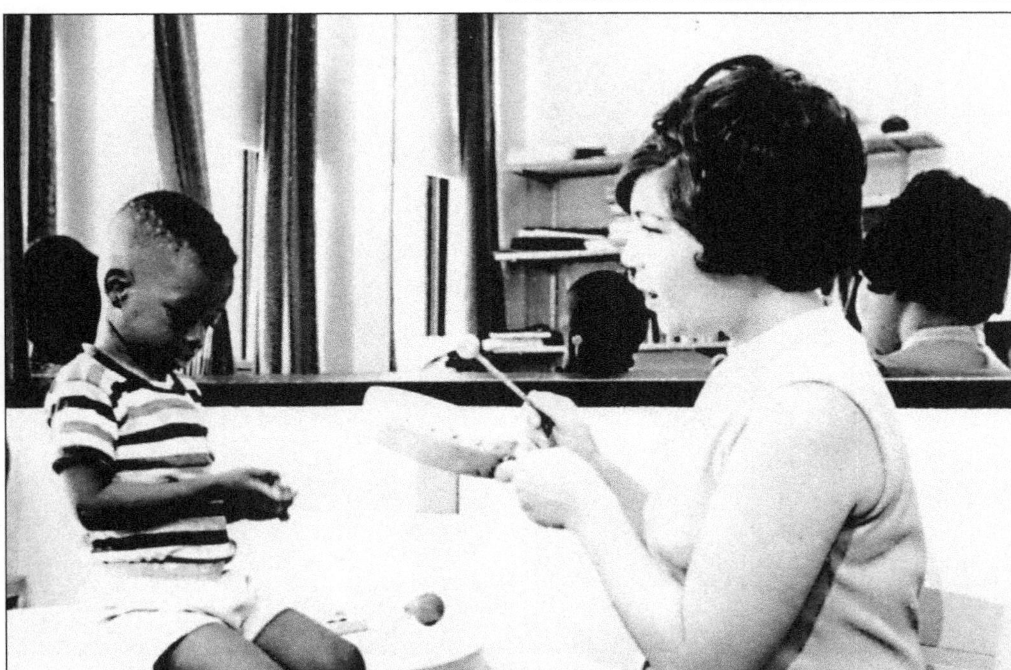

AN AUDIOLOGY EXAMINATION. Children's Hospital expanded its services in the Otolaryngology Department by merging with the Sarah Fuller Foundation and establishing a speech and hearing clinic. Here, a child takes a hearing test.

A Senatorial Visit. U.S. senators from Massachusetts Edward M. Kennedy (left) and John F. Kerry (right) have been frequent visitors to Children's Hospital. They have worked closely with the Office of Child Advocacy to pass legislation to advance the hospital's mission of providing the best possible care to all children.

A Royal Visit, 1986. A child has the opportunity to greet the future king of England when Prince Charles (second from left) visits Children's Hospital. Diagnosed with acute lymphoblastic leukemia, the patient underwent chemotherapy and an autologous bone marrow transplant, which helped him become the healthy nine-year-old shown here.

DR. C. EVERETT KOOP, 1989. Many distinguished visitors have come to Children's Hospital to give guest lectures. Pictured here is Dr. C. Everett Koop (center), then U.S. surgeon general and former trainee at Children's Hospital Boston, who became chief of pediatric surgery at Children's Hospital of Philadelphia.

CHILD LIFE SERVICES, 2001. Support for patients and families is central to pediatric care, and specialists work with hospitalized children to enhance their recovery. Shown here is Myra Fox, longtime director of Child Life Services, with Curious George and friends on the anniversary of the publication of *Curious George Goes to the Hospital*, by Margaret and H. A. Rey. Fox had guided the Reys around Children's Hospital 35 years before and was the model for the "play lady" in the book.

THE MARTHA ELIOT CHILD HEALTH CENTER. Children's Hospital has always had a major commitment to care for Boston's underserved children. In 1967, the Martha Eliot Health Center opened in the city's Roxbury neighborhood, shown above. The photograph below, taken in 2001, shows the improved facility that opened in 1996.

THE COMMUNICATIONS CENTER, 1978. Children's administrator Lendon Snedeker wrote in 1969, "Hospitals cannot live by Chiefs alone, nor by research laboratories, nor even Nobel Prize winners." Countless individuals work behind the scenes to make Children's Hospital what it is. Shown here are operators long before the days of cellular phones and pagers.

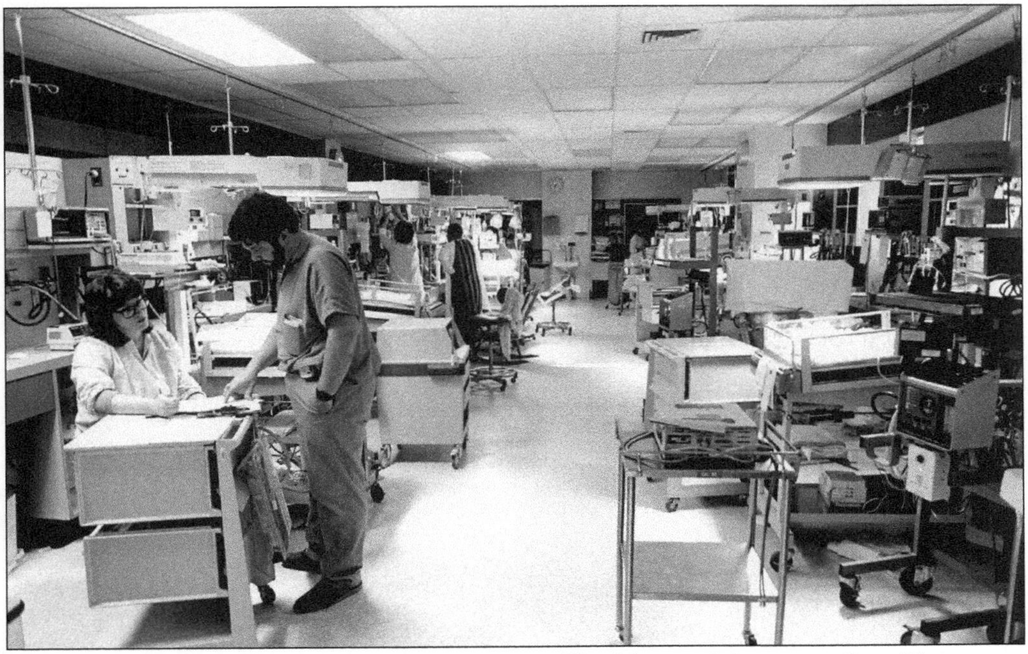

THE NEONATAL INTENSIVE CARE UNIT, 1987. The Neonatal Intensive Care Unit treats the youngest and smallest patients referred to Children's Hospital. As the number of patients increased and the use of advanced technology expanded, space to care for patients became severely limited.

THE MAIN BUILDING, 1987. Children's Hospital entered a new phase of its history in 1987 with the completion of a new inpatient facility (center). This 10-story building enabled the hospital to provide inpatient care for 325 patients and became the first segment of an expansion program that propelled Children's Hospital into the 21st century.

Six

LOOKING FORWARD

THE 1990S AND BEYOND

The 1990s through the present have been years of increasingly expert patient care, great research productivity, and growing medical innovation at Children's Hospital Boston. The complexity of care increased as powerful drugs and space-age technology helped to better diagnose and treat children who previously had no hope. The hospital's core philosophy of providing the most advanced pediatric care while continuing to push the boundaries for new treatments has led to countless scientific and medical breakthroughs during this period.

In terms of patient care, Children's Hospital's pioneering work has included double lung transplantation for a patient with cystic fibrosis; partial liver transplants from parents to children; multiple-organ system transplants in infants; surgery using robotics, lasers, and intra-operative MRI; development of tissue-engineered organs; promising treatments for sickle cell anemia; the invention of a tiny device to repair holes in hearts without invasive surgery; and fetal interventions for hypoplastic left heart syndrome and other congenital conditions.

In the laboratory, Children's Hospital researchers are making tremendous contributions to the understanding and future treatment of blood disorders; regeneration of damaged nerves; identification of the genes that play a critical role in disease, including the specific gene responsible for the most common form of muscular dystrophy; clarifying molecular mechanisms of health and disease; and development of a vaccine against *haemophilus influenzae*, one of the most common bacterial infections affecting young children. The new field of angiogenesis is a classic example of where the hospital's unusual strength in basic sciences leads to the development of exciting and promising new therapies.

Children's Hospital has come a long way from its birth in a townhouse on Rutland Street. Its International Center helps families from more than 100 nations receive advanced care not available in their home countries. Each year, interpreters assists tens of thousands of families, speaking more than 40 languages, to receive care. The Chaplaincy and Social Services Programs offer support 24 hours a day to thousands of children and families whose beliefs are rooted in traditions from around the world.

Today, Children's Hospital Boston is a complex organization that maintains its original aims: giving the most advanced pediatric healthcare; discovering the causes of pathology and disease; educating the best future medical leaders; and advocating for children's health. As long as children need healing, Children's Hospital Boston will help.

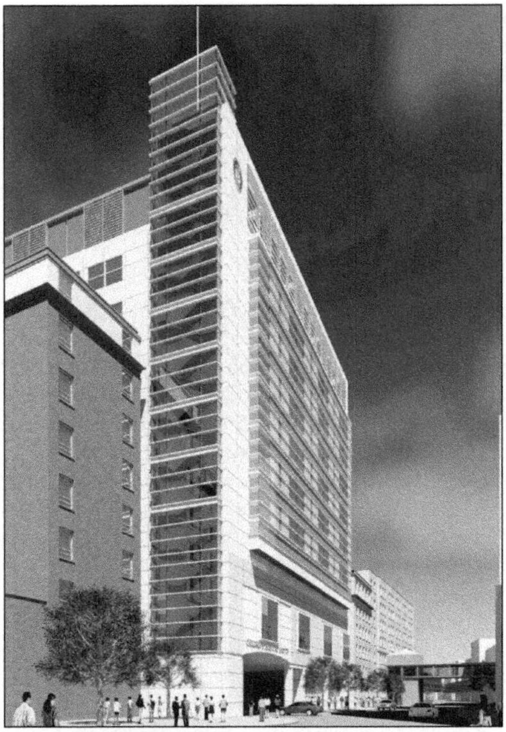

A New Clinical Building, 2005. The hospital must deal creatively with the constant need for additional facilities. A new clinical building (shown in this architectural proposal) was constructed on the site of the former Carnegie Building. It added 250,000 square feet to the campus and created new intensive care units, operating rooms, cardiac catheterization laboratories, and space for other much needed medical and surgical beds and equipment. (Courtesy Visarc, from Shepley Bulfinch Richardson and Abbott, Architects.)

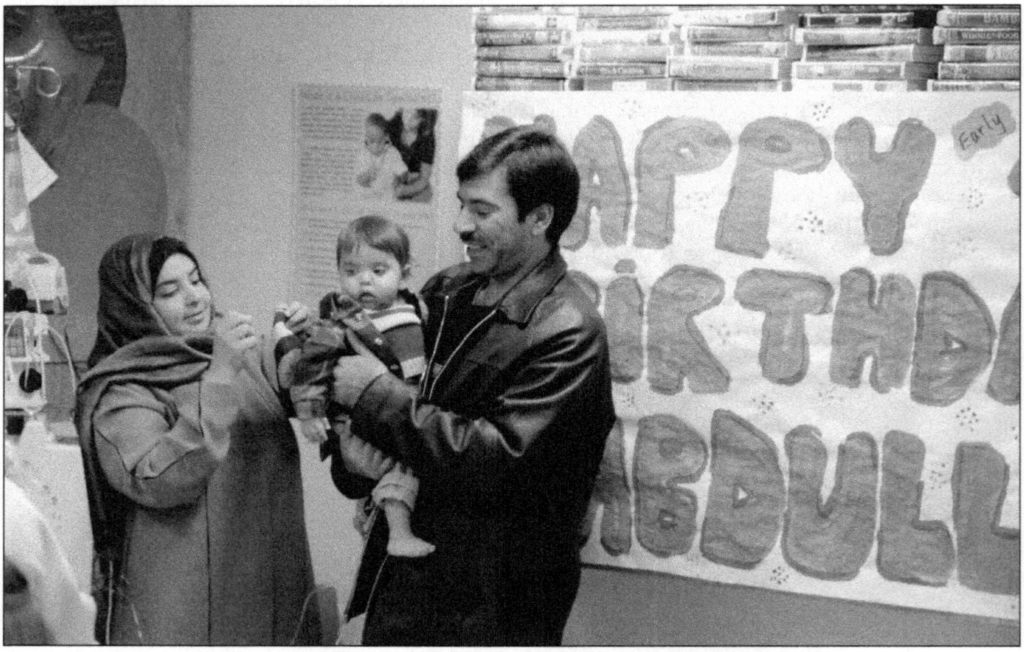

Patients from around the World, 2004. Children's Hospital provides care for patients from around the country and the world who come for treatment unavailable closer to home. Here, a child and his family are pictured on the occasion of his first birthday, celebrating successful transplantation of his liver, bowel, pancreas, and stomach.

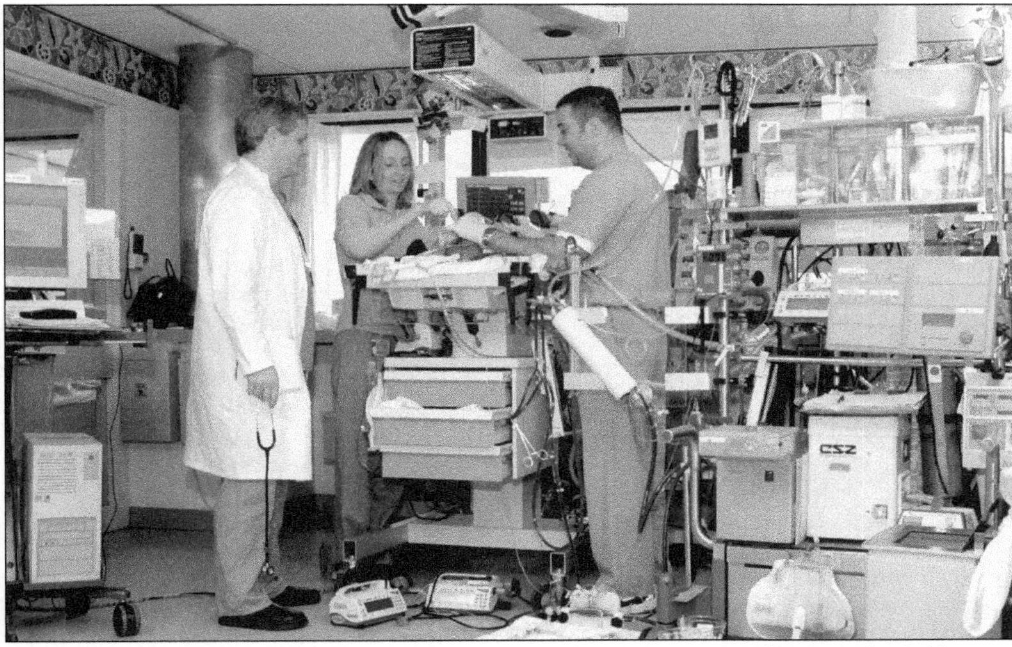

ECMO IN THE ICU, 2005. As medical care has become more sophisticated, children are treated for formerly fatal conditions. This child is on extra-corporeal membrane oxygenation (ECMO), a technique used to manage severe cardio-respiratory failure. Highly skilled nurses, respiratory therapists, and other specialists are necessary to provide such complex care.

THE ECMO SURVIVORS REUNION, 2004. On the 20th anniversary of the Children's Hospital's ECMO program, patients who survived gathered for a celebration. The date also happened to be the third anniversary of the 2001 terrorist attack. Dr. Jay Wilson, surgical director of the ECMO program, remarked at the time, "On September 11, we honor those who aren't here but should be. Today, we're also celebrating those patients who are here but shouldn't be."

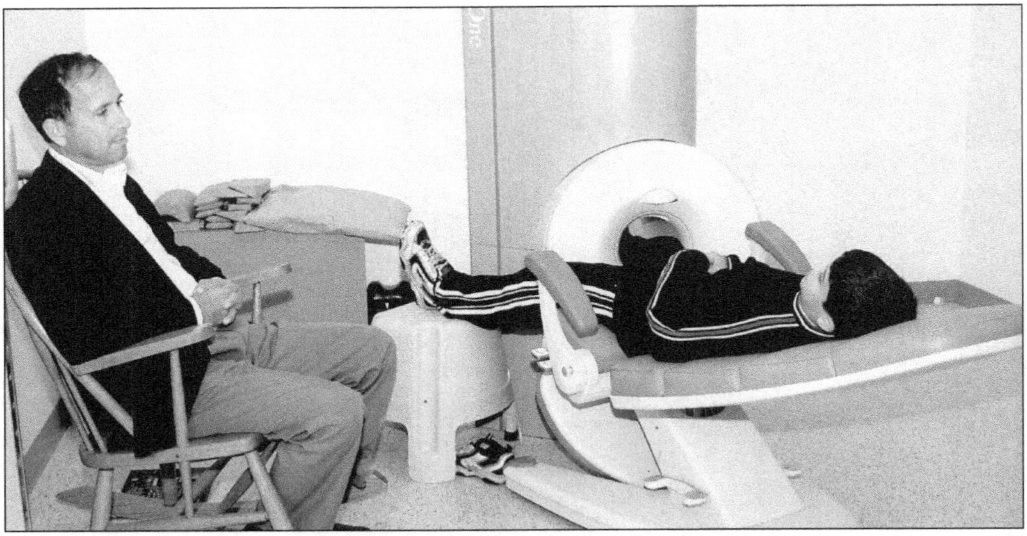

New Diagnostic Equipment. These powerful, versatile, high-tech machines include the CT scan (computerized tomography), MRI (magnetic resonance imaging), and PET scan (positron emission tomography). The pictured MRI scanner is designed specifically for extremities, avoiding the need to confine a child inside a full-body machine. Each of these diagnostic tools can reveal or "image" different internal structures or processes of the human body. They can also detect a variety of diseases such as cancerous tumors, vascular disorders, and bone abnormalities.

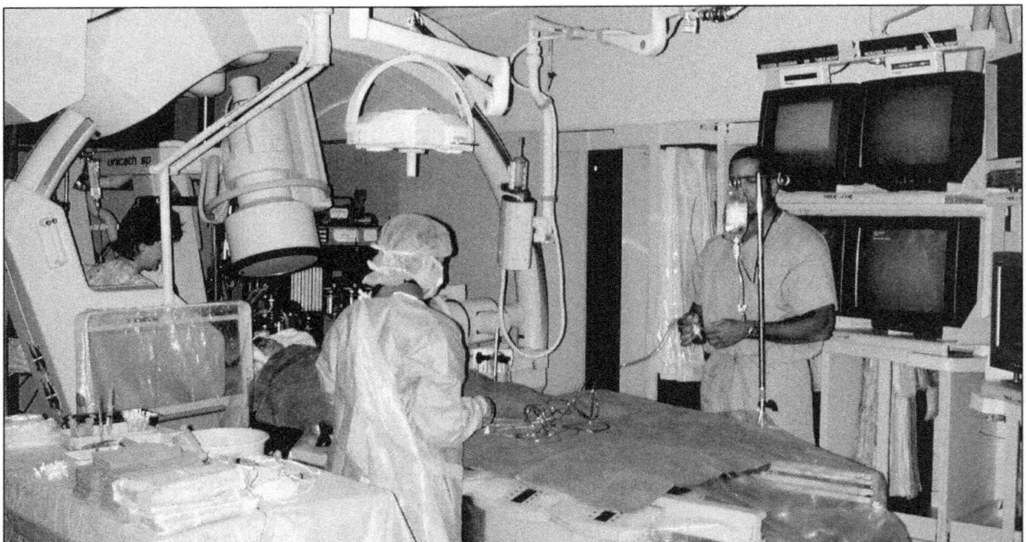

The Cardiac Catheterization Laboratories, 2004. Technological advances have touched every aspect of medicine, perhaps nowhere more impressively than in the cardiac catheterization laboratory. Modern imaging equipment enables cardiologists to perform diagnostic and therapeutic procedures that have had a major impact on children with congenital heart disease. Some anomalies that previously required surgery can now be treated much less invasively in the catheterization laboratory.

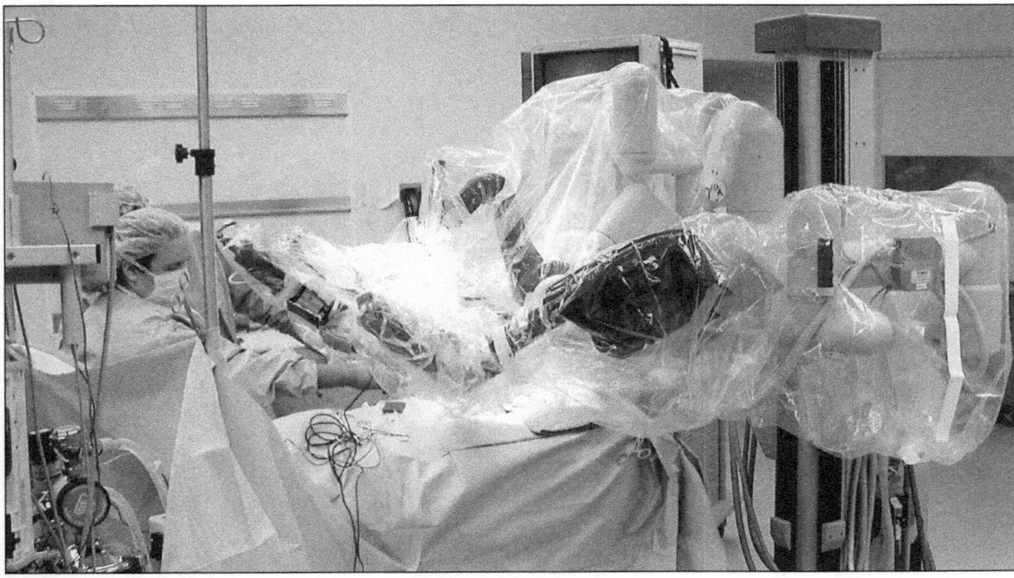

SURGICAL ROBOTICS, 2004. Technological advances have been enormous in recent years. Shown here is a robotic system facilitating urologic surgery, although it has been used for other surgical procedures as well. It enables surgeons to perform increasingly complex operations on very young patients through very small incisions. (Courtesy Craig Peters, MD.)

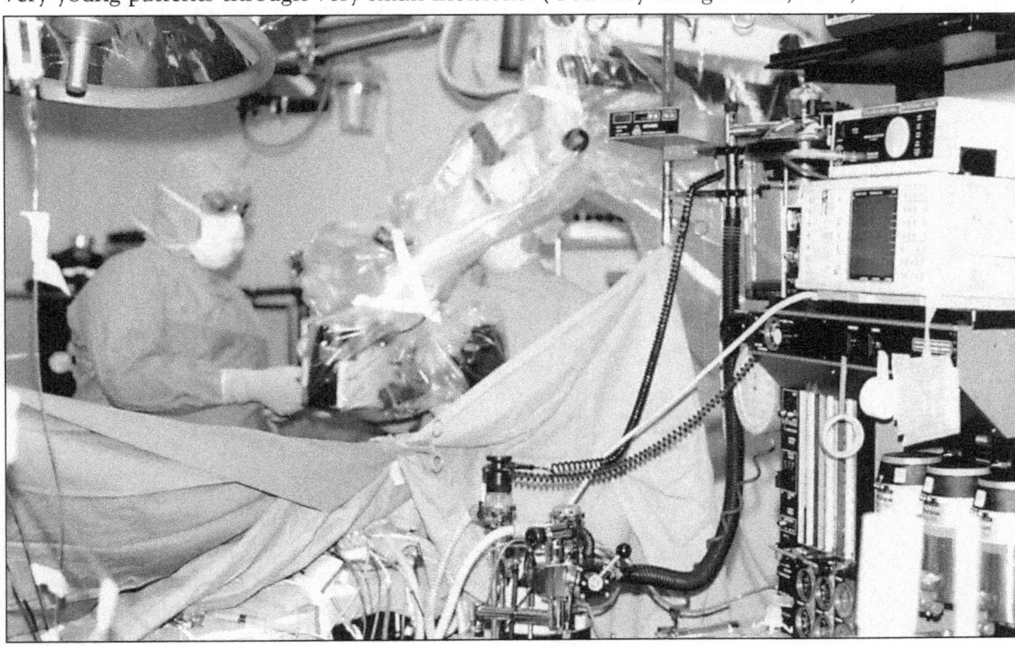

MODERN ANESTHESIA AND SURGERY. Surgical procedures of a complexity unimaginable years ago are now regularly performed. This is due, in part, to advanced technology and much safer, more sophisticated anesthesia management. Only the patient's small hand is visible here (lower center), under the surgical drapes, while a high-powered microscope is used during a delicate operation. Anesthesiologists and intensivists now provide care and pain treatment during and after surgery for children throughout the hospital, not just in the operating rooms.

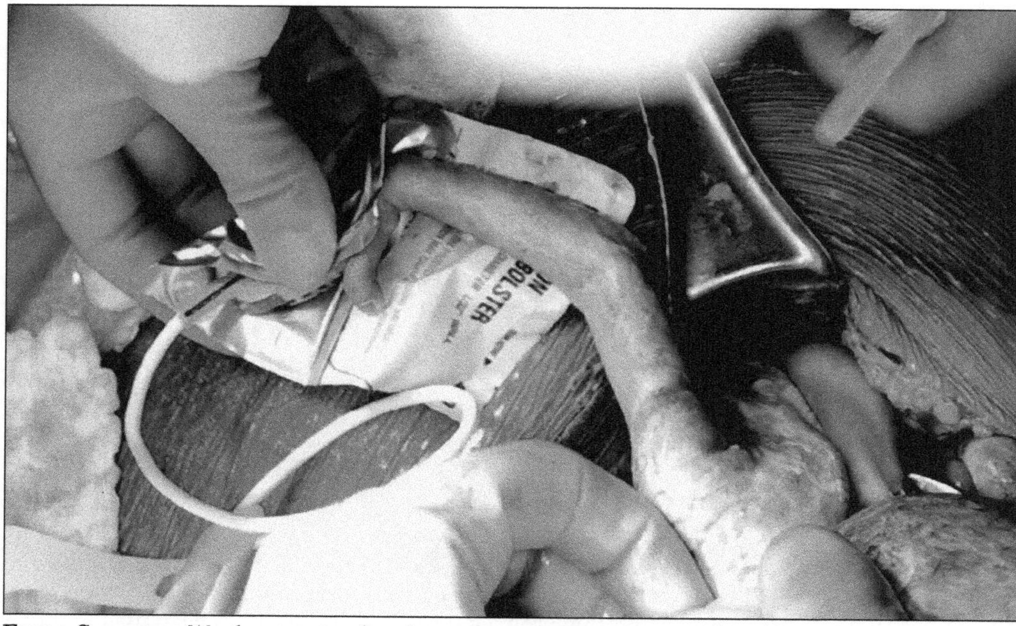

FETAL SURGERY. Much attention has focused on treating congenital problems as early as possible in order to provide the best outcome for an entire lifetime. Seen here is a monitoring device being attached to the arm of a fetus prior to fetal surgery. (Courtesy Russell Jennings, MD.)

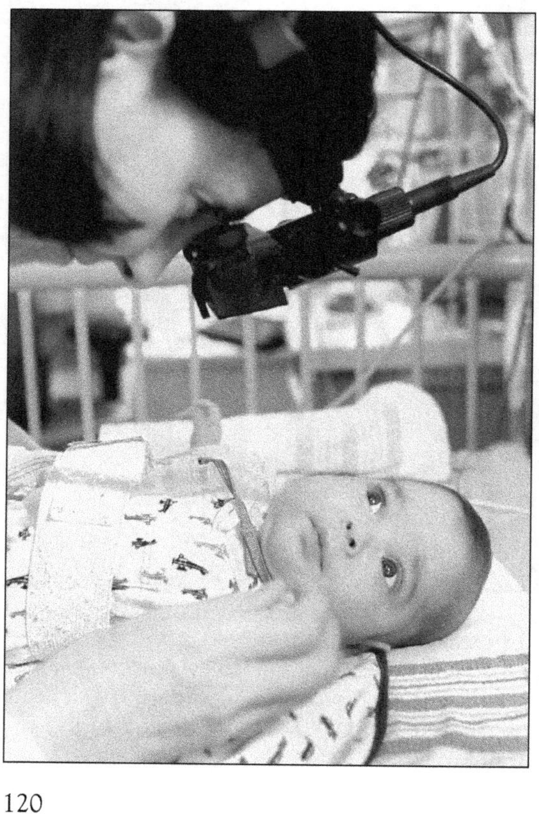

FROM THE BENCH TO THE BEDSIDE. Linking research with clinical care has been a hallmark of Children's Hospital since its founding. One example of this is in the field of ophthalmology, as seen here, a department headed for more than 30 years by Dr. Richard Robb. Laboratory research attempts to perfect new techniques for prevention and treatment of the visual problems that sometimes develop in extremely premature babies. (Courtesy Paula Lerner.)

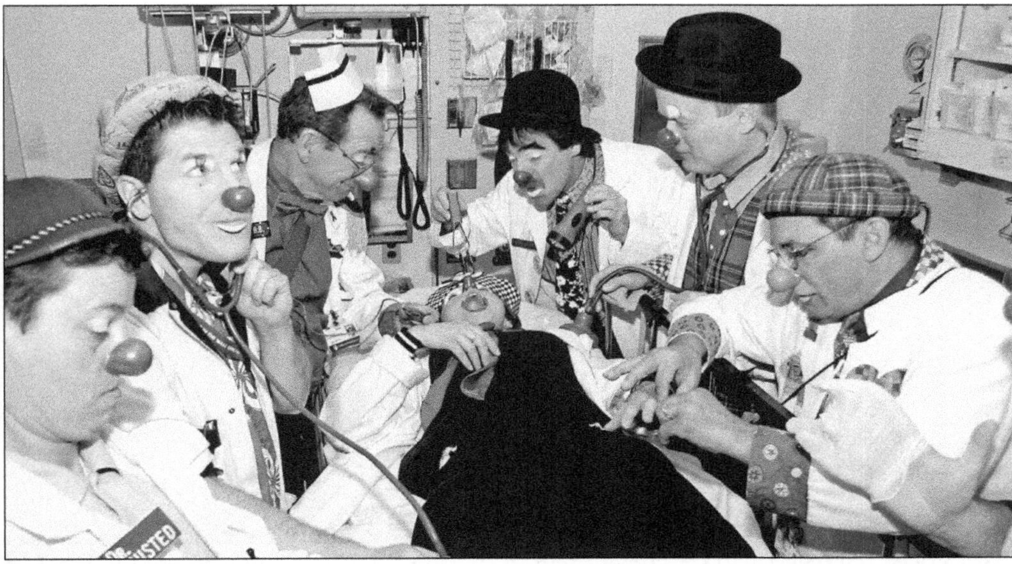

"SEND IN THE CLOWNS." If laughter is the best medicine, Children's Hospital certainly provides it. The Big Apple Clown Program brings bedside clowning humor and diversion to patients, their families, and staff members. These clowns, traveling in pairs, carry physicians' black bags bulging with red noses, jars of bubbles, rubber chickens, and musical instruments. When going on "Clown Rounds," they "prescribe" laughter and good humor as the universal treatment. (Courtesy George Taylor, MD.)

INFORMATION TECHNOLOGY. The hospital staff uses new, emerging technologies to brighten the lives of patients and their families and to increase their comfort. Providing access to the resources of the Internet enhances communication and education. TLContact and the hospital's CarePage permit patients and their families to design Web pages to spread news and photographs to friends and family far away. School-age patients may also access the Internet to keep up with their homework via interactive online learning programs.

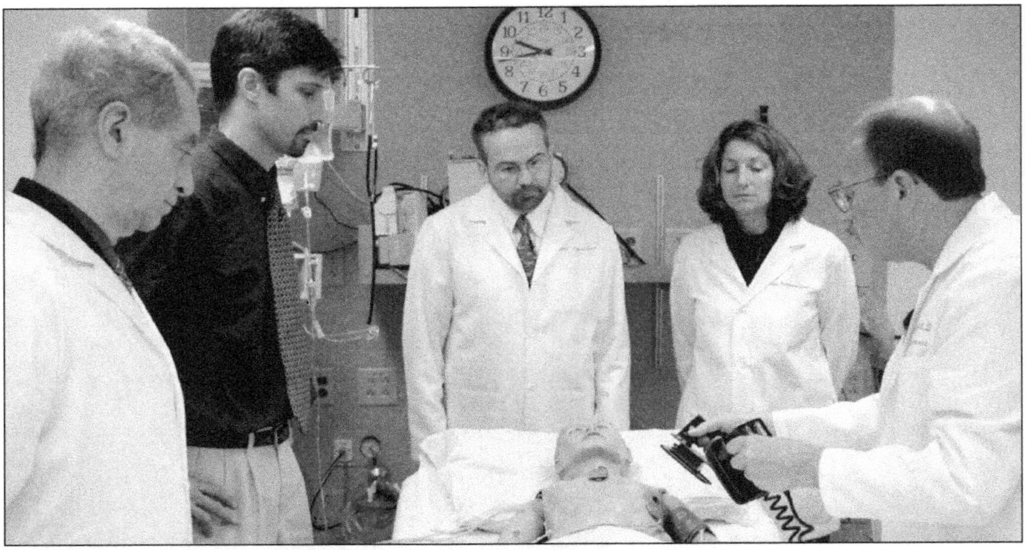

Simulation Training, 2005. Opened in 2002, the Simulator Suite is one of the first critical care training facilities in a pediatric hospital in the United States. It continues to provide a setting for practicing lifesaving procedures and teamwork during resuscitation of pediatric patients. A new state-of-the-art mannequin, with physiologically based responses to interventions and medications, can create lifelike critical care situations for training staff. This technology helps provide the best possible training and patient care.

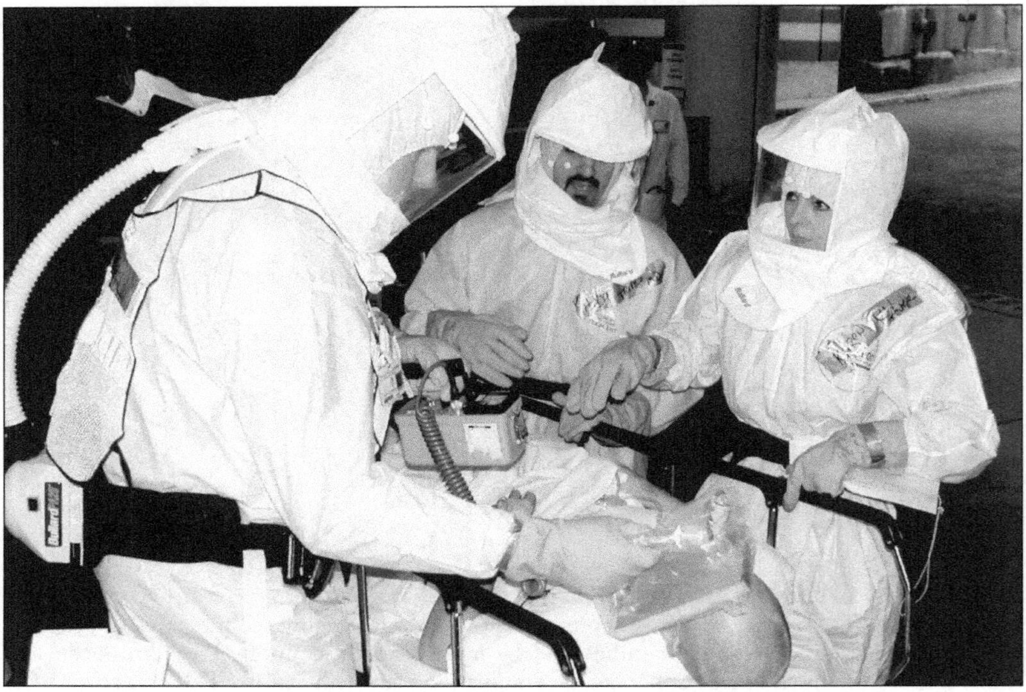

Preparation in Uncertain Times. This photograph shows a bio-terrorism training session at Children's Hospital. The hospital actively prepares its staff to deal with victims of biological, chemical, or radiological injury.

THE GROWING HOUSE STAFF. Today, all hospital departments have residents and fellows who spend from a few months to multiple years learning how to care for children. The impressive number of physicians in training in any given year is apparent in the above photograph of the 2003 house staff in the Department of Medicine. Many house officer physicians remain on the staff at Children's Hospital after completing their training, while others take prominent positions in other hospitals in the United States or abroad. Below, Dr. W. Hardy Hendren (first row, center) appears in 1997 with his past chief residents as they celebrate his long service as chief of general surgery. (Photograph by Bachrach.)

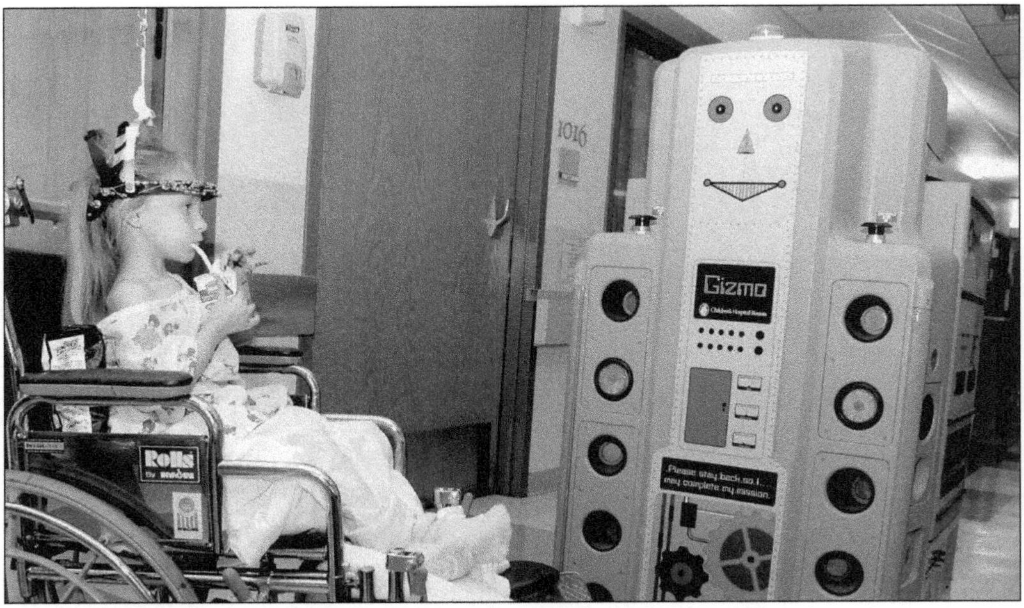

A Robot Named Gizmo. This mechanical wizard stands five feet tall and weighs a mere 600 pounds. Gizmo, named in a hospital-wide contest in 2002, can carry up to 200 pounds and runs errands for the medical records office. Gizmo may be the only hospital "employee" who works a round-the-clock schedule seven days a week.

The Karp Family Research Laboratories. Already home to the world's largest pediatric research enterprise, Children's Hospital nearly doubled its research space with the opening of the Karp Building in 2003. With 12 stories of light-filled atria and spacious laboratories, the building is designed to foster a free-flow of ideas among scientists working across many disciplines. The Karp Research Building houses more than one million zebra fish that have become a key animal model for studying many genetic diseases in humans. (Courtesy Robert Benson.)

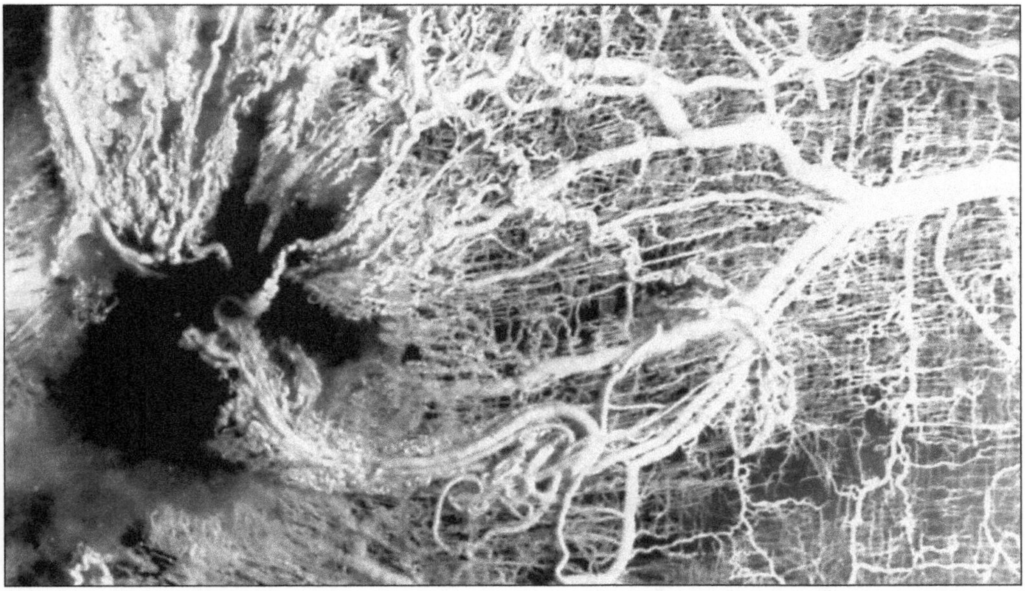

Vascular Biology. Vascular biologists study many pathological conditions that involve the growth of abnormal blood vessels (as seen here), a field pioneered by Children's Hospital surgeon Dr. M. Judah Folkman. These conditions include most types of cancer; degenerative eye diseases, including diabetic retinopathy and macular degeneration; and chronic inflammatory diseases, such as rheumatoid arthritis and psoriasis.

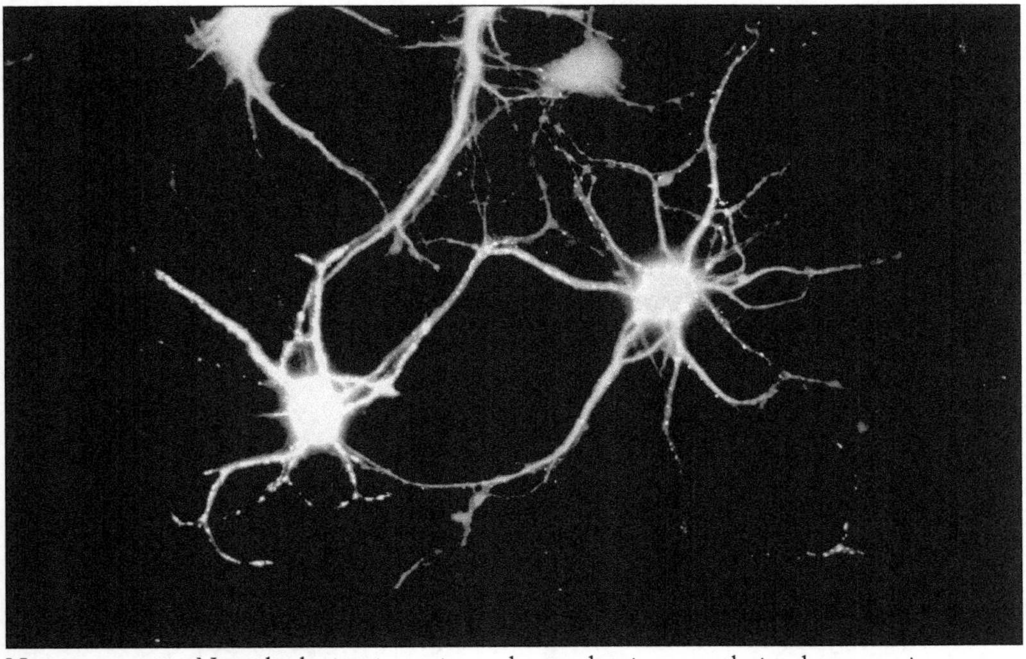

Neurobiology. Neurobiologists investigate the mechanisms regulating key steps in nervous system development. One goal is to increase understanding of nervous system disorders affecting children. Staff members also train the next generation of physician scientists in both molecular and developmental neurosciences.

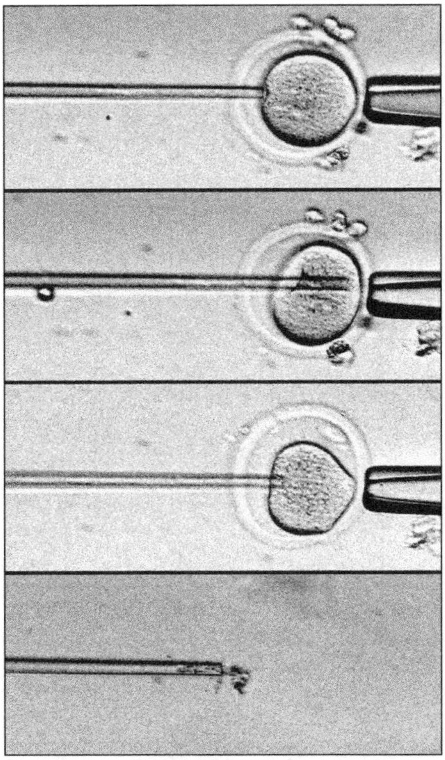

Developmental Biology. The pictured technique is used to generate customized stem cells. Stem cells are generic cells with potential to differentiate into cells possessing the properties of specific organs or tissues. Developmental biologists study how stem cells affect human development and may be used to treat diseases such as diabetes, muscular dystrophy, heart abnormalities, anemias, and even spinal cord injuries.

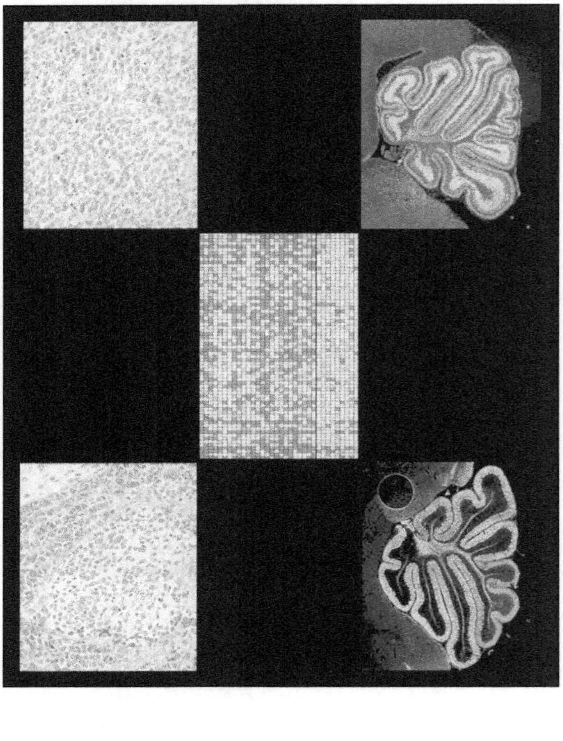

The Genomics and Informatics Programs. The Genomics Program builds on newly discovered information from the sequencing of the human genome. Greater knowledge of genomics has the potential to predict the likelihood of future diseases as infants and children develop. The Informatics Program uses techniques from biology, medicine, mathematics, and computer science to analyze and interpret the growing volume of information derived from "high-tech" genomics. Research projects also analyze data from conditions as diverse as asthma, autism, cancer, diabetes, and heart disease in children. (Courtesy Scott Pomeroy, MD.)

Children's Hospital Boston

Statistical Report, FY 2003

Patients	**2003**	**2002**
Number of licensed beds	322	324
Discharges	17,291	16,431
Patient days		
Inpatient days	93,557	92,001
Observation days	4,743	4,586
Total Patient days	98,300	96,587
Average stay in days	4.46	4.60
Ambulatory visits		
Clinic visits	250,982	253,964
Foundations visits	128,322	114,152
Emergency services visits	51,006	52,288
Total ambulatory visits	430,310	420,404

Tests and procedures	**2003**	**2002**
Surgical procedures		
Inpatient	6,909	6,974
Outpatient	13,863	13,079
Total surgical procedures	20,772	20,053
Personnel		
Active medical and dental staff	860	849
Affiliate medical staff	43	33
Associate scientific staff	287	268
Emeriti	93	93
House staff	773	631
Nursing staff	978	903
Other full-time equivalent employees	4,299	4,071
Active volunteers	470	445

Recent Hospital Statistics. A quick comparison of recent hospital statistics with the first annual report from 1869 (see chapter 1) demonstrates the remarkable growth of the institution. This is a strong testament to the vision of the hospital founders and the ongoing mission of Children's Hospital Boston.

The Children's Hospital Boston Time Capsule, 2003. To honor the hospital's rich history, a time capsule was dedicated in the hospital lobby. Staff members and patients chose memorabilia representing contemporary hospital work. The time capsule will be opened in 2069 to mark the hospital's 200th anniversary. Although some of the objects will be obsolete, the hospital's commitment to care for children in the most effective, modern ways will endure.

An Aerial View, 2003. This photograph shows the Longwood Medical area packed with buildings—educational, research, and clinical. It is one of the largest concentrations of its kind in the world, bringing together thousands of the most talented clinicians and researchers. The leaders of Children's Hospital planned well in moving the small but growing hospital close to Harvard Medical School. Children's Hospital's prime location, virtually in the center of the medical complex, has made it a high-visibility hub of pediatric medicine and surgery. (Courtesy On the Fly Aerial Photography, Don Varney.)

CPSIA information can be obtained
at www.ICGtesting.com
Printed in the USA
BVHW011646130922
646905BV00003B/19

9 781531 622138